The Future of Business Credit:

AI, Blockchain, and the New Rules of Business Lending

PUBLISHED BY Ember Maple Editions

Ember Maple Editions – C. Stonebook

Table of contents

Introduction

For centuries, access to credit has been the lifeblood of commerce. From the handwritten ledgers of Renaissance bankers to the sophisticated underwriting algorithms of modern financial institutions, the idea remains the same: a business's ability to grow hinges on its ability to borrow. And yet, the rules of this game—who gets credit, how much, at what cost, and with what risk—have been dictated by centralized systems, opaque evaluation methods, and a heavy reliance on outdated assumptions.

But today, those rules are on the brink of a complete transformation.

We are standing at the threshold of a credit revolution unlike anything the business world has ever seen. Artificial intelligence, blockchain technology, and the rise of decentralized finance are not just buzzwords—they are powerful forces that are rewriting the blueprint of how credit is granted, monitored, and managed. This transformation isn't happening in the distant future; it's unfolding right now, in ways both subtle and seismic.

Traditional credit models—built on legacy systems and limited data—are rapidly being challenged by a new ecosystem of technologies that see more, understand more, and adapt faster. These innovations are not merely making the old systems more efficient; they're redefining the very logic behind business lending. Suddenly, the constraints that once held back small entrepreneurs, early-stage startups, or unconventional business models are falling away. Credit is no longer a gate guarded solely by banks and credit bureaus. It's becoming something more accessible, dynamic, and intelligent.

This shift has not happened overnight. Rather, it is the product of decades of gradual technological evolution—made more urgent by recent global disruptions that exposed the fragility of the financial system. The COVID-19 pandemic, for example, highlighted just how ill-equipped many traditional lenders were to assess risk in real time. Businesses that had strong digital footprints but weak credit histories were left in the cold, while others with long-standing relationships received funding despite declining relevance. In the aftermath, it became clear: a new approach to credit assessment was not just desirable—it was necessary.

Enter AI-driven credit scoring. Rather than relying on a narrow band of financial metrics, modern algorithms now have the capacity to process vast quantities of alternative data—everything from cash flow trends and transaction histories to social media engagement and real-time operational metrics. These tools aren't replacing human judgment entirely, but they are augmenting it in profound ways. Lenders are now empowered to see deeper into the day-to-day realities of a business's health, not just its historical record. This shift toward predictive, behavior-based modeling is upending the longstanding supremacy of traditional credit scores.

But the revolution doesn't stop with better analysis. Blockchain is fundamentally reengineering the infrastructure of lending itself. With smart contracts, decentralized ledgers, and immutable transaction histories, blockchain introduces a level of transparency and trust that centralized systems have long struggled to achieve. Businesses can now access credit marketplaces where funding is instantaneous, terms are coded into the protocol, and collateral is managed without intermediaries. This new landscape reduces friction, lowers costs, and creates opportunities for both borrowers and lenders who were previously left out of the game.

Consider the rise of decentralized finance (DeFi), which operates entirely outside the conventional banking system. These platforms are already enabling peer-to-peer business lending, where capital flows across borders without the need for banks, underwriters, or even human intervention. While still in its early stages, the DeFi movement represents a dramatic rethinking of how credit can work when technology—not institutions—is the trusted intermediary.

Of course, these changes come with challenges. Regulatory frameworks have not yet caught up with the velocity of innovation. Questions around data privacy, algorithmic bias, and systemic risk loom large. There is a very real danger that, without thoughtful governance, new technologies could replicate or even exacerbate the inequities of the old system. The tools may be different, but the outcomes could remain the same—unless we build systems that are not only more intelligent but also more equitable and accountable.

That's one of the central concerns this book aims to address. It's not enough to marvel at the potential of AI and blockchain; we must also grapple with the implications. Who owns the data? Who audits the algorithms? How do we ensure that access to credit becomes more inclusive rather than more selective? These are not hypothetical questions. They are at the heart of the decisions being made in boardrooms, startups, policy think tanks, and regulatory agencies around the world right now.

And they matter to every business owner—whether you're running a family restaurant, launching a tech startup, managing a growing e-commerce brand, or overseeing a mid-sized manufacturing firm. Because in the near future, your access to capital won't be determined by your relationship with a local banker or the score in your credit file. It will be shaped by how well your business is digitally understood, how seamlessly your data can be verified, and how trustworthy your operations appear in a transparent and programmable financial ecosystem.

This is not science fiction. It's happening already.

Banks are partnering with fintechs to integrate real-time cash flow analytics into their lending decisions. Invoice financing is being automated through blockchain-backed smart contracts. AI is being used to detect fraudulent applications with greater accuracy than ever before. Alternative lenders are offering capital to businesses in underbanked regions, using mobile data and transaction histories as the basis for decision-making. In short, the future of business credit is arriving—fast.

Yet for many entrepreneurs and even financial professionals, the speed of change can feel overwhelming. The tools are evolving so rapidly that it's difficult to know where to begin. That's why this book exists—not to offer vague forecasts or speculative trends, but to provide a grounded, comprehensive roadmap for navigating this transformation.

We'll start by tracing the history of business credit, understanding how we got here and why the legacy system was ripe for disruption. From there, we'll explore the core technologies powering the shift—from machine learning to distributed ledgers—and see how they're being applied in real-world lending scenarios. We'll examine the players reshaping the space, from scrappy fintech disruptors to forward-thinking regulators and institutional giants. And we'll dig into the risks, the ethical questions, and the emerging best practices that will shape the next generation of business finance.

Most importantly, we'll center this discussion on practical implications. What do these shifts mean for the small business owner applying for a line of credit? For the CFO of a mid-market enterprise evaluating funding options? For the investor deciding where to place their trust—and their capital—in a decentralized world?

Because the credit revolution isn't just about abstract systems or flashy tech. It's about people. It's about entrepreneurs who need funding to bring their visions to life. It's about communities that thrive when small businesses have the resources to grow. It's about a global economy that becomes more resilient and innovative when access to capital is no longer a bottleneck, but a bridge.

As you read through these pages, one thing will become clear: the future of business credit is not a single destination, but an evolving frontier. It will demand adaptability, strategic thinking, and above all, a willingness to challenge the status quo. Whether you're a technologist, a banker, a business owner, or simply a curious observer of financial evolution, this book is your invitation to engage with what's coming—and to prepare for a financial landscape that looks nothing like the past.

We are entering an age where business credit is no longer a matter of paperwork and waiting periods. It's a world of data-driven insights, instant verification, and programmable trust. The foundations of business finance are being rebuilt from the ground up. What comes next will redefine how businesses grow, how risks are managed, and how opportunities are unlocked.

The credit revolution is at our doorstep. The question is: are you ready to walk through?

Chapter 1: The Death of Traditional Credit Scoring

1.1 The FICO Monopoly Crumbles

For decades, the three-digit FICO score stood as the unchallenged gatekeeper of financial access in the United States. Developed by the Fair Isaac Corporation in 1989, the FICO score quickly became the industry standard for evaluating creditworthiness across mortgages, auto loans, credit cards, and increasingly, business credit. What was once a revolutionary tool—a standardized, quantitative way to assess risk—transformed into a rigid and exclusionary metric that defined who got credit, how much they received, and on what terms. But that dominance is now under siege.

The unraveling of FICO's monopoly is not the product of a single event but rather the result of technological shifts, changing consumer expectations, evolving data ecosystems, and the emergence of a new philosophy around financial inclusion. To understand why this crumble was inevitable, we must first understand how the FICO model embedded itself so deeply in the financial fabric—and why it is no longer enough.

FICO scores were built on a relatively narrow set of data points: payment history, credit utilization, length of credit history, new credit inquiries, and types of credit used. For a long time, this model offered a workable proxy for risk. But it was also inherently limited. It required a track record of traditional credit activity—credit cards, loans, and installment payments—to even exist. For millions of people and businesses operating outside the conventional financial system, this meant invisibility. No score, no loan. No loan, no growth.

This rigidity affected small business lending even more starkly. Many small businesses, particularly those just starting out or operating in cash-heavy sectors, lacked formal credit histories. Their FICO scores—if they existed at all—were often tied to the personal credit of the founders. This blurred line between personal and business credit created risk not just for the borrower but also for lenders, who had no granular visibility into the actual health or potential of the business.

And yet, banks and financial institutions leaned heavily on this score as a filtering mechanism. A FICO score below a certain threshold? Automatic rejection. An exceptional score? Approval with favorable terms. This approach, while efficient from a processing standpoint, neglected nuance. It penalized those with thin credit files, failed to account for short-term volatility, and ignored important indicators like cash flow consistency, customer loyalty, or operational efficiency.

By the late 2010s, the cracks were beginning to show. Fintech startups began questioning the dogma of credit scoring. Why should someone who pays their rent and utilities on time every month be considered high-risk simply because they don't use credit cards? Why should a business with steady sales and healthy cash reserves be denied funding because its owners had minimal personal borrowing history?

These questions gave rise to a new wave of credit modeling— one that looked beyond the FICO framework and toward alternative data. Platforms like Square Capital, Kabbage, and PayPal Working Capital began underwriting loans using data drawn directly from transaction histories, point-of-sale systems, and real-time revenue metrics. These lenders didn't care about a business's FICO score; they cared about how money was flowing in and out of the business now. The result? Faster approvals, better fit products, and access for borrowers previously shut out by the system.

But this was just the beginning. As artificial intelligence and machine learning entered the picture, the limitations of traditional credit scoring became even more obvious. Algorithms could now analyze thousands of variables in real time—inventory turnover, social sentiment, payroll consistency, customer retention rates— and paint a far more accurate picture of risk than five retroactive categories ever could.

Suddenly, the FICO score seemed less like a comprehensive assessment and more like a relic of a pre-digital era.

The 2020 global pandemic became a turning point. In the chaos of early lockdowns, when traditional risk models failed to account for unprecedented volatility, lenders who had relied solely on FICO were caught flat-footed. Businesses with impeccable credit scores were collapsing overnight. Others, deemed high-risk by conventional models, pivoted quickly, adapted their operations, and not only survived but thrived. Lenders with alternative underwriting models were better positioned to identify these resilient borrowers. And borrowers took note.

This shift in borrower behavior accelerated the FICO decline. Entrepreneurs began gravitating toward platforms that offered not just faster approval, but smarter evaluation. They were tired of being punished for circumstances outside their control—like a missed utility bill five years ago or a lack of credit card usage. They wanted credit decisions based on who they were now, not what a formula decided years ago.

Meanwhile, regulators began opening the door to more inclusive models. The Consumer Financial Protection Bureau (CFPB) started encouraging the use of alternative data, recognizing its potential to bring underserved populations into the credit fold. Pilot programs were launched, partnerships formed, and suddenly, what was once considered "non-traditional" began entering the mainstream.

Even major players started hedging their bets. In 2019, FICO released the UltraFICO score, a belated attempt to incorporate bank account data into its models. It was a tacit acknowledgment that the traditional system was no longer sufficient. But the damage had already been done. The mystique of the all-powerful FICO score had been punctured. In its place, a new vision of creditworthiness was taking root—one that valued context over history, behavior over assumptions, and real-time data over retroactive snapshots.

Businesses themselves began to rethink their financial identities. Rather than focusing on building traditional credit profiles, they invested in data transparency—integrating their accounting platforms, streamlining payments, and sharing operational metrics with lenders through APIs. What emerged was a new kind of borrower: one that was not only more visible to lenders but more in control of how they were perceived.

This power shift marked the beginning of the end for FICO's monopoly. While the score still plays a role—particularly in consumer lending and institutional underwriting—its grip is loosening. It is no longer the sole currency of trust. A business's ability to access credit is increasingly dependent on its data footprint, not its adherence to traditional metrics.

As we move further into the digital age, the implications are profound. Lenders are no longer bound to rigid credit tiers. Borrowers are no longer at the mercy of a number they can't fully influence. And the ecosystem of credit—long dominated by centralization and bureaucracy—is becoming more dynamic, personalized, and open.

That doesn't mean the transition will be smooth. FICO is deeply embedded in the infrastructure of finance. Mortgage underwriting, credit card approvals, and even certain business loan structures still hinge on it. But the tide is turning. The old model is slowly but surely giving way to a future that is more data-rich, more equitable, and more adaptable.

This chapter in the story of business credit is not just about one company losing its hold. It's about a deeper transformation in how we think about risk, opportunity, and trust. The FICO monopoly didn't collapse in a single day. It is crumbling piece by piece—challenged by innovation, undermined by changing expectations, and replaced by models that see the full complexity of a borrower's financial life.

In the chapters to come, we will explore how this collapse is making room for something better—credit systems powered by artificial intelligence, blockchain-backed transparency, and decentralized platforms that redefine the boundaries of access. But it all starts here, with the unraveling of a system that once seemed unshakeable. The FICO score may still be on the books, but its reign is ending—and the future of business credit is wide open.

1.2 Beyond Payment History: The Data Revolution

The reliance on payment history as the cornerstone of credit evaluation once made sense in a world where information was limited, digital infrastructure was rudimentary, and financial relationships followed traditional patterns. If a person or a business paid their bills on time, month after month, year after year, it was assumed they were trustworthy. In this linear framework, consistency equated to reliability, and missed payments were red flags. But as the global economy shifted into the digital age, this approach began to show its cracks.

Today, data flows continuously from an ever-growing web of sources. Businesses leave behind intricate digital footprints that go far beyond invoices and bank statements. Ecommerce platforms log every transaction. Inventory systems record real-time supply chain activity. Customer reviews, marketing engagement, click-through rates, and even employee turnover metrics tell stories about the health and potential of an enterprise. In this new landscape, relying solely on payment history is like trying to navigate a city using a map from the 1800s—it doesn't reflect the reality of where businesses operate or how they evolve.

The data revolution began quietly, seeded by the rise of cloud computing and digital finance platforms that turned once-private ledgers into open, analyzable streams. Platforms like QuickBooks, Xero, Stripe, and Shopify created ecosystems where financial performance wasn't something that needed to be reconstructed or interpreted—it was available in real time, often down to the minute. Suddenly, lenders didn't have to wait for quarterly reports or rely on backward-looking metrics. They could plug directly into a business's financial machinery and observe the pulse of its operations as they happened.

This opened the door to a new class of underwriting. Instead of basing risk on what a borrower had done, lenders could begin to ask what the borrower was currently doing and how that behavior aligned with success. A business that had late payments a year ago might now show steady cash flow and month-over-month growth. Another with perfect past payment behavior might show signs of stagnation, a drop in customer activity, or rising refund rates. Traditional scoring models would never catch this nuance, but data-rich systems could.

The shift didn't just allow for better decisions—it enabled faster ones. The old process of gathering tax returns, combing through bank statements, and waiting on personal guarantees gave way to API connections, instant verification, and dynamic analysis. For businesses operating in fast-moving sectors, this was a game changer. A seasonal product brand, for example, could demonstrate its viability through pre-order volumes and fulfillment efficiency, not just its bank balance. A service provider could highlight customer churn rates and client acquisition velocity as indicators of sustainability.

This change was particularly meaningful for startups and small businesses—segments often penalized by thin files or short operational histories. These enterprises might not have the years of financial paperwork required by traditional lenders, but they had something better: streams of real-time data that revealed how they operated, how they responded to challenges, and how they engaged with their customers. That data, when harnessed correctly, proved far more predictive than payment history alone.

It's important to recognize that this data revolution wasn't simply a matter of quantity—it was a qualitative transformation. Information once seen as peripheral or even irrelevant to credit decisions became central. Shipping delays, website uptime, employee satisfaction scores, and even social media engagement patterns began to feed into new models of risk assessment. These indicators, often overlooked by traditional systems, provided early warnings or green lights that told a deeper story about operational integrity and future viability.

Financial institutions began to recognize the potential. Banks, credit unions, and alternative lenders raced to integrate data aggregation tools and partner with fintech platforms that could enhance their visibility into a borrower's world. Open banking initiatives accelerated this trend, mandating the secure sharing of financial data with third-party providers upon customer consent. In this open environment, businesses were no longer locked into static profiles. They could curate their financial identities, highlight their strengths, and differentiate themselves from competitors through transparency.

Of course, this abundance of data raised critical questions around privacy, consent, and data governance. Not all data is equally relevant, and not all usage is ethical. As the pendulum swung toward hyper-personalized underwriting, regulators and consumer protection advocates stepped in to ensure that data usage remained fair, explainable, and non-discriminatory. Still, the overall trajectory was clear: the more data a business could safely share, the more nuanced and accurate their risk profile became.

What emerged from this revolution was a new paradigm: dynamic creditworthiness. No longer fixed to a score frozen in time, a business's access to credit began to reflect the fluid reality of its day-to-day existence. Just as streaming services tailor recommendations in real time, so too did lenders begin adjusting terms, limits, and offers based on up-to-date data. Credit became less of a binary decision—approve or deny—and more of a responsive system attuned to context.

At the heart of this change was a shift in philosophy. Traditional models viewed creditworthiness as a test of past behavior. The new models viewed it as a living signal—a series of ongoing patterns that could be tracked, interpreted, and acted upon. This reconceptualization laid the groundwork for the next major evolution in business lending: behavioral credit models.

1.3 The Rise of Behavioral Credit Models

As data expanded in scope and accessibility, the question for lenders shifted from "What happened?" to "What is likely to happen next?" This pivot—subtle at first—gave rise to a wave of behavioral credit models that focus not only on outcomes, but on the processes and tendencies behind them.

Behavioral credit models represent a radical departure from legacy scoring. They are not based on what a borrower has achieved in terms of balances or payments. Instead, they examine how a borrower operates. How does a business manage its cash flow? How consistent are its invoices? How quickly are obligations met, even under strain? How do decision-makers react to external pressures or market shifts? These are behavioral questions, and answering them requires both granular data and interpretive frameworks that can process complex patterns.

The origins of behavioral modeling can be traced to other sectors, especially insurance and advertising. Insurers long ago began using behavioral data—such as driving habits recorded by telematics devices—to determine risk and set premiums. Advertisers, likewise, built entire platforms around tracking consumer behavior to predict purchases and personalize content. Credit, by contrast, had been slow to adapt—bound by regulatory inertia and institutional conservatism.

But that began to change when AI and machine learning entered the underwriting equation. These tools made it possible to ingest large amounts of behavioral data and identify correlations that would be invisible to the human eye. A business that responded quickly to customer inquiries, maintained steady supplier relationships, and avoided frequent overdrafts began to exhibit the behavioral profile of a low-risk borrower—even if its traditional credit history was sparse or volatile.

One of the most powerful aspects of behavioral models is their predictive capacity. Rather than waiting for missed payments or declining revenues, these models flag warning signs early— offering a chance to intervene, restructure, or support the borrower before a crisis deepens. This proactive stance not only reduces losses for lenders but also fosters healthier relationships between financial institutions and the businesses they serve.

Another key advantage is resilience. Behavioral models can continue functioning even in uncertain environments where historical data becomes unreliable. During the early months of the pandemic, for example, many traditional models failed to anticipate business failures or spot recovery trends. Behavioral models, on the other hand, detected adaptation efforts—like curbside service rollouts, subscription pivots, and digital marketing investments—that signaled agility and growth potential.

These models also adapt to the natural variability of different business types. A seasonal business, which might look unstable on a monthly cash flow statement, can show strong behavioral patterns of savings buildup and smart off-season planning. A new business, lacking long-term history, can still demonstrate discipline, growth intent, and market responsiveness.

The shift toward behavior-based credit analysis has also created new incentives for businesses. Just as drivers became more cautious when monitored by insurance apps, entrepreneurs began to manage their operations with greater awareness, knowing that their day-to-day choices could impact their credit prospects. This feedback loop encouraged more sustainable practices, better financial hygiene, and a clearer understanding of what lenders value in the modern era.

Yet the transition hasn't been without its growing pains. The use of behavioral data has stirred debates about fairness and transparency. How are these models trained? Are they biased toward certain industries or practices? Can borrowers understand what behaviors are being evaluated and why? To address these concerns, some lenders have adopted "explainable AI" models—systems designed to make their decisions interpretable and challengeable. This transparency has become essential in building trust and ensuring ethical use of emerging tools.

As behavioral credit models continue to evolve, they are reshaping the entire ecosystem of small business finance. From microloans in developing economies to venture debt in the startup world, underwriting is becoming more fluid, adaptive, and real-time. Lenders who once relied on quarterly reviews or annual credit updates now operate in near-continuous engagement with their borrowers, adjusting exposure and support based on the latest behavioral signals.

The ultimate outcome is a more human-centered approach to credit. Paradoxically, as technology takes a larger role in lending decisions, the understanding of borrower behavior becomes more nuanced, personal, and empathetic. Lenders no longer rely on black-box scores. They observe, interpret, and respond—like partners, not just creditors.

In this model, trust is not assumed based on past transactions. It is built through ongoing behavior. And that shift—more than any single tool or platform—is what will define the future of business credit.

Chapter 2: AI-Powered Underwriting: The New Decision Makers

2.1 Machine Learning Algorithms Replace Human Intuition

For centuries, lending decisions were deeply personal. A business owner would walk into a local bank, sit across from a loan officer, and present a case. That officer—armed with experience, financial statements, and a feel for the borrower—would make a judgment. This process was far from perfect. It could be biased, slow, inconsistent, and heavily influenced by subjective factors like personal rapport or risk aversion. But at its core, underwriting was a human art form: a mixture of instinct, knowledge, and institutional policy.

That era is rapidly fading.

Today, the most influential decisions about business lending are no longer made in a room by a person. They are made in milliseconds by algorithms that weigh thousands of variables, test them against historical outcomes, and calculate risk with a level of speed and complexity far beyond human capability. This shift, while subtle on the surface, represents one of the most transformative changes in financial history: the replacement of human intuition with machine learning in the domain of credit underwriting.

Machine learning (ML) is not just another buzzword in finance. It's a functional shift in how creditworthiness is understood, processed, and acted upon. Traditional underwriting relied on linear thinking—if income is X, debt is Y, and collateral is Z, then the likelihood of default is within range A. These models were often based on manually weighted formulas or decision trees. They were slow to adapt and heavily reliant on institutional assumptions. Machine learning, by contrast, allows systems to learn from vast datasets, recognize patterns, adjust parameters in real time, and constantly refine their predictive accuracy.

At the core of this evolution is the idea that risk is not static—it's dynamic, contextual, and behavioral. Rather than viewing a borrower through five or ten variables, modern algorithms assess hundreds or even thousands. They draw from structured data like bank statements, tax filings, and balance sheets, and unstructured data like email cadence, website activity, inventory turnover, or customer feedback. All this information is processed and interpreted by the algorithm not as isolated facts, but as interconnected signals that reveal deeper truths about business operations.

One of the most compelling advantages of machine learning is its ability to detect non-obvious correlations. A human underwriter might note that a business has three late utility payments and assume financial instability. An algorithm might observe that those late payments coincide with a seasonal revenue dip that historically rebounds within two months and that overall vendor payments remain consistent—signaling temporary fluctuation, not systemic risk. What appears risky at first glance may, in light of hundreds of other factors, be well within the acceptable range.

This level of granular analysis gives lenders a powerful edge. Approval rates go up because more borrowers can be evaluated accurately. Default rates go down because risk is calculated with better precision. Processing times are slashed from days or weeks to seconds. And small businesses, which often operate in unpredictable environments, are finally assessed on their real-world complexity rather than simplified metrics.

Crucially, machine learning models are not static. They improve over time. Each loan issued—successful or not—feeds back into the system as new training data. The model recalibrates, refining its predictive capabilities with every decision it makes. This continuous learning loop creates underwriting systems that evolve in tandem with economic conditions, industry shifts, or borrower behavior trends. In contrast, traditional models remain frozen until manually updated, often lagging behind the realities of the market.

Take, for instance, a business that operates in a niche ecommerce space. It might use multiple payment processors, run ad campaigns with fluctuating ROI, and sell seasonally influenced products. To a human underwriter unfamiliar with the nuances of the sector, the numbers may appear inconsistent or risky. But an algorithm trained on similar businesses in the same category can recognize the patterns. It knows what a healthy account looks like during peak season, what ad conversion rates predict sustained revenue, and what inventory cycles signal overextension or growth. The machine learning system isn't simply checking boxes—it's interpreting signals within a living, breathing ecosystem.

This is the foundation of intelligent underwriting: credit decisions that reflect context, not just criteria.

It also means that lenders can create specialized models for different industries, geographies, or borrower types. A restaurant in Manhattan is not evaluated the same way as a SaaS company in Austin or a home services provider in rural Ohio. Each business has its own rhythm, its own data profile, and its own risk markers. With machine learning, underwriting is no longer one-size-fits-all. It's adaptive, modular, and context-sensitive.

Beyond risk prediction, AI-driven underwriting has also introduced a new level of explainability—often referred to as "model interpretability." Early versions of AI in finance were criticized for their "black box" nature: they produced results, but it was hard to understand why. Today, thanks to advancements in interpretable machine learning, we can now trace how specific inputs—such as a spike in vendor payments or changes in customer acquisition costs—contributed to a credit decision. This transparency is essential not only for compliance and regulation but also for borrower trust. Businesses want to know why they were denied credit, what they can improve, and how they were evaluated. AI systems can now provide those answers with clarity, helping borrowers take actionable steps.

Still, the transition has not been universally welcomed. There are valid concerns. Algorithms, after all, are only as unbiased as the data they're trained on. If historical data reflects systemic inequalities or skewed access to credit, machine learning models can perpetuate those patterns unless carefully audited and corrected. That's why responsible AI underwriting includes not just technical excellence but also ethical oversight—monitoring models for fairness, inclusion, and unintended consequences.

This is especially important for small businesses owned by minorities, women, or immigrants—groups that have historically been underserved or misrepresented in financial systems. The promise of AI is not just better accuracy, but also better equity. To achieve that, models must be tested for disparate impact, trained on diverse datasets, and constantly evaluated for fairness. Lenders who fail to address these dimensions risk reinforcing the very barriers they claim to overcome.

Another issue is explainability versus performance. The most accurate models are often the most complex, involving neural networks and ensemble methods that are hard to decipher. In regulated environments, particularly in countries with strict financial laws, this complexity can be a liability. That's why some lenders are choosing hybrid models—pairing machine learning systems with rule-based overlays or human review stages. The goal isn't to remove humans from the process entirely, but to augment their judgment with powerful tools.

Indeed, in the best systems, human analysts don't disappear—they evolve. They shift from gatekeepers to interpreters. Rather than spending time on rote data entry or mechanical decision-making, they focus on edge cases, exception handling, and customer engagement. They review flagged applications, adjust policy thresholds, and use the insights generated by AI to make more informed, strategic decisions. This hybrid approach combines the empathy and contextual awareness of humans with the scalability and pattern recognition of machines.

What's particularly exciting about this transition is the accessibility it brings. Once upon a time, advanced underwriting tools were the domain of multinational banks with billion-dollar R&D budgets. Today, even small lenders or fintech startups can integrate open-source machine learning libraries, leverage cloud-based AI services, and access shared datasets to build intelligent credit systems. This democratization of underwriting technology is accelerating innovation and forcing legacy institutions to evolve or be left behind.

In emerging markets, AI-powered underwriting is even more revolutionary. In regions where credit bureaus are sparse, formal credit histories are rare, and banking infrastructure is limited, machine learning models trained on mobile phone usage, utility payment behavior, or agricultural patterns are enabling loans to first-time borrowers. These models don't just fill gaps—they redefine what it means to be creditworthy in a digital-first world.

And as embedded finance grows—where lending is integrated directly into software platforms, ecommerce checkouts, or vendor portals—the role of machine learning becomes even more central. Credit decisions happen behind the scenes, in real time, often triggered by a user action. There's no time for paperwork or phone calls. Everything must be instant, seamless, and accurate. This is only possible when underwriting itself is autonomous, intelligent, and deeply integrated into the digital fabric of commerce.

The age of AI-powered underwriting is not a vision of the future. It is already here, operating across industries, continents, and borrower types. It is redefining speed, reshaping standards, and rebalancing power. Machine learning has not merely replaced human intuition—it has restructured the decision-making process from the ground up. Credit is no longer based on what a person remembers, assumes, or believes. It's based on what the data reveals, in all its depth and complexity.

As we move forward, the challenge will not be whether AI can underwrite effectively—that has already been proven. The challenge will be ensuring that these systems remain fair, transparent, and aligned with human values. The algorithms may decide, but we must still guide the direction. Because while machine learning has replaced intuition, it has not replaced responsibility. That remains ours.

2.2 Real-Time Risk Assessment Engines

The traditional rhythm of credit evaluation followed a predictable pattern: gather documents, wait for processing, and receive a decision days—or even weeks—later. This system, while functional for much of the twentieth century, is increasingly misaligned with the demands of today's business environment. Companies move fast. Markets shift in hours, not quarters. In this new landscape, the idea of static credit evaluations feels not just outdated, but dangerously inadequate. That's where real-time risk assessment engines come into play, redefining the tempo and depth of modern lending decisions.

At its core, real-time risk assessment is about immediacy—evaluating a borrower's creditworthiness not on stale metrics, but on the living, breathing data of the present moment. It's not enough to know that a company met its obligations last month or had a profitable quarter. Lenders want to understand what's happening right now: how much cash is flowing in today, what expenses are due tomorrow, and whether there are early signs of stress or resilience. Real-time systems make this visibility possible by connecting directly to the digital infrastructure businesses already use—accounting platforms, bank feeds, point-of-sale systems, payment processors, logistics dashboards, and more.

Instead of pulling snapshots, these engines stream data continuously. A business's receivables aren't reviewed once a year—they're monitored daily. Inventory levels, vendor payments, customer reviews, and employee churn rates become part of a dynamic evaluation profile. When risk models ingest this stream of information, they don't just make a judgment based on aggregate figures. They detect trends, anomalies, and behavioral cues that indicate where the business is headed in the hours and days ahead.

This continuous monitoring is especially powerful in volatile environments. A business impacted by a sudden supply chain disruption or a viral product launch can see its risk profile change dramatically in a short period. Traditional systems might overlook these shifts until the next statement is submitted or an overdue payment triggers concern. Real-time assessment, by contrast, identifies the change as it happens—flagging risk, adjusting credit exposure, or even triggering proactive outreach from the lender.

The implications are enormous. Lenders can recalibrate exposure automatically. If a borrower's risk profile improves, their credit line can be expanded without them needing to apply. If warning signs appear—such as a decline in sales velocity or a spike in late invoice payments—the system can reduce exposure, offer renegotiation terms, or initiate a review before a default occurs. Credit becomes fluid and responsive, governed by algorithms capable of subtlety and speed.

For borrowers, this model introduces a new paradigm. They are no longer forced to prove their worthiness once and hope for the best. Instead, their operational behavior continuously communicates their risk level. If they manage cash wisely, pay vendors on time, and show steady growth, the system recognizes and rewards those patterns. This feedback loop incentivizes sustainable financial behavior, making real-time systems not just evaluative, but developmental.

The architecture of these engines is built on several layers. First comes data integration—ensuring a seamless connection between the lender and the borrower's systems. APIs, cloud-based accounting, and standardized data formats have made this easier than ever. Next comes the risk model itself—typically a machine learning algorithm trained on millions of data points across industries, geographies, and borrower types. But the real innovation lies in the orchestration layer: the part of the system that turns insight into action. This is where policy thresholds are embedded, where alerts are triggered, and where credit decisions are implemented automatically.

A retail business that experiences a surge in sales, for instance, might see its inventory depleted quickly. A real-time engine notices this shift in product turnover, sees that restocking is imminent, and—based on historic fulfillment reliability—decides to extend an advance on future earnings. The entire process, from signal to funding, can happen in minutes, not days.

This speed doesn't just make things more efficient—it enables entirely new types of credit products tailored to immediate needs.

Real-time risk engines also enhance fraud detection. By observing patterns across multiple data streams, the system can detect inconsistencies that a human analyst might miss. If a business claims high sales volume but shows no corresponding shipping activity, or if supplier payments remain flat despite reported expansion, these discrepancies raise red flags. The system flags them instantly, allowing further investigation before disbursing funds.

Such engines also improve portfolio management for lenders. Instead of reviewing loans quarterly or annually, risk managers can monitor exposures daily. They can segment borrowers into dynamic cohorts based on behavioral trends, sector-specific risks, or even external events such as weather disruptions or economic policy changes. This allows for real-time rebalancing of risk, reducing the chances of systemic failures.

Critics of automated assessment worry about the depersonalization of lending. But real-time systems don't replace the relationship; they enhance it. By freeing human analysts from repetitive reviews, these engines allow them to focus on strategic engagement—working with businesses that need support, customizing solutions, and helping borrowers interpret their data. The machines handle the detection; the people handle the dialogue.

Still, challenges remain. Real-time risk assessment relies on data accuracy and integrity. A misconfigured API, a syncing delay, or a data anomaly can skew outputs. Lenders must invest in robust data validation, fallback systems, and human oversight to ensure reliability. Moreover, transparency is essential. Borrowers should understand what is being tracked, how it's interpreted, and how they can influence it. This requires clear communication and, in some cases, dashboards that reflect the borrower's risk posture in real time.

Despite these challenges, the trajectory is undeniable. In a world where business can be won or lost in a week, lenders can no longer afford to work with delayed insights. Real-time engines offer a future where credit is adaptive, predictive, and supportive—not just a gatekeeper, but a partner in the borrower's journey. The logic of credit has shifted from static judgments to living assessments. And in that shift, opportunity has expanded for both sides of the equation.

2.3 Explainable AI for Regulatory Compliance

As artificial intelligence takes center stage in underwriting and credit risk modeling, one question rises above all others: can we trust these systems to make decisions that are fair, accountable, and transparent? For all their power and precision, machine learning algorithms face a critical test—not just in performance, but in explainability. In the world of finance, where regulatory oversight is strict and the consequences of bias or error can be severe, explainable AI (XAI) has emerged as both a technical necessity and a moral imperative.

At the heart of this challenge is a paradox. The most powerful AI models—the ones that deliver the greatest predictive accuracy— are often the most opaque. These so-called "black box" systems, such as deep neural networks or ensemble models, make decisions that are difficult to interpret even for data scientists. They work, but they don't always reveal why they work. In consumer applications, this may be acceptable. But in lending, where decisions impact people's livelihoods, businesses' futures, and the stability of financial systems, opacity is a risk.

Regulatory bodies around the world have taken note. In the United States, the Equal Credit Opportunity Act (ECOA) and Fair Lending laws require lenders to provide specific reasons for credit denials. The General Data Protection Regulation (GDPR) in Europe enshrines the right to an explanation for automated decisions. In other words, if an algorithm decides to deny credit to a small business, the borrower has the right to know why. This requirement has placed enormous pressure on financial institutions to adopt models that are not only accurate but also interpretable.

Explainable AI addresses this need by making machine learning decisions understandable to humans. This doesn't mean dumbing down the model or sacrificing performance. It means designing systems that can articulate the factors that led to a decision, show how different variables influenced the outcome, and provide a clear rationale that can be audited and challenged if necessary. It's about turning statistical logic into actionable insight.

There are multiple ways to achieve explainability. Some models are inherently transparent, such as decision trees or linear regression. These are easy to interpret but may lack the sophistication needed for complex credit analysis. Others use post hoc techniques—tools that analyze black box models after the fact to extract explanations. Examples include SHAP (Shapley Additive Explanations) and LIME (Local Interpretable Model-Agnostic Explanations), which identify which variables had the greatest impact on a specific decision.

These techniques allow lenders to provide meaningful disclosures. A borrower denied credit can be told, for instance, that their revenue volatility, late invoice payments, and declining customer retention were key factors. More importantly, they can be shown how addressing these areas might improve their chances in the future. This transforms the credit decision from a mysterious verdict into a constructive conversation.

Explainable AI also enables internal governance. Risk officers, compliance teams, and auditors need to understand how models behave across populations. Are they systematically disadvantaging businesses in certain regions? Are they skewed against certain business models or sectors? With XAI, institutions can perform fairness tests, monitor bias drift, and enforce model discipline. They can ensure that decisions are not just legal, but ethical and consistent with corporate values.

This level of transparency becomes even more crucial as AI-driven decisions expand into embedded finance, where credit is issued within ecommerce platforms, gig economy apps, or vendor marketplaces. In these contexts, borrowers may not even realize they are being evaluated by an algorithm until they're accepted or denied. Explainability ensures that the automated systems making these decisions remain accountable, traceable, and challengeable.

However, implementing explainable AI is not without cost. There is often a trade-off between model complexity and interpretability. Striking the right balance requires collaboration between data scientists, legal teams, business leaders, and ethicists. It also requires investment in tooling, documentation, and governance frameworks that support responsible AI use.

But the rewards are substantial. Explainable systems build trust—with borrowers, with regulators, and within the institution itself. They enable continuous improvement, as errors can be traced and corrected. They support inclusivity, by identifying where bias may unintentionally emerge. And they future-proof lending operations against tightening regulatory standards, which are likely to demand ever-greater transparency in the years ahead.

In the end, explainable AI is not a technical feature—it is a foundational principle of ethical credit. It affirms the idea that automation does not mean abdication of responsibility. On the contrary, it means assuming greater responsibility, because the decisions made by machines have real-world consequences. The future of business credit lies not just in smarter systems, but in systems that can be understood, questioned, and improved. That is the true promise of AI—not just intelligence, but wisdom.

Chapter 3: Blockchain's Immutable Credit History

3.1 Decentralized Credit Bureaus: Trustless Verification

The modern credit system, for all its institutional grandeur, has long been predicated on centralized trust. Banks, lenders, and regulators have placed their faith in a handful of credit bureaus to record, store, and interpret the financial behavior of individuals and businesses alike. These agencies—transnational in reach yet limited in transparency—have historically operated as gatekeepers to credit access, aggregating data from lenders and furnishing scores that dictate who gets a loan, on what terms, and under what conditions. For decades, the system worked well enough, but its flaws were always visible to those who looked closely.

Errors in reports, opaque algorithms, identity mismatches, and unilateral decision-making plagued the experience of millions. Small business owners were often forced to rely on personal credit scores to secure funding, despite running solvent enterprises. Newcomers to the financial system—whether immigrants, young entrepreneurs, or micro-businesses in developing economies—were rendered invisible, not because they were untrustworthy, but because the system lacked mechanisms to verify their existence. Centralized credit bureaus, for all their data, were still gatekeepers of exclusion.

Now, blockchain is rewriting that equation entirely.

At the core of blockchain technology lies a simple but revolutionary principle: trustless verification. In a blockchain network, trust does not need to be placed in a single institution, company, or administrator. Instead, verification is handled collectively and cryptographically across a decentralized ledger. Every transaction, once validated and written to the chain, becomes immutable—a permanent record accessible to all participants. This innovation—initially conceived for digital currencies—has profound implications for the world of credit.

Imagine a credit system where no single institution controls the data, where credit history isn't stored in a walled garden but distributed across a peer-to-peer network, where verification does not depend on permission, but on consensus protocols and cryptographic proof. That's the vision behind decentralized credit bureaus—networks built on blockchain infrastructure that enable credit history to be recorded, validated, and accessed without centralized intermediaries.

In this emerging system, credit data is not aggregated and stored in one central database. Instead, it is logged on a distributed ledger, where each transaction—each repayment, each loan disbursement, each fulfillment of a financial obligation—is recorded as a block in the chain. The identity of the borrower, verified through decentralized identity systems, is tied to a cryptographic key rather than a vulnerable Social Security number or a proprietary file. This means no single entity can modify or erase history. Fraud, manipulation, and error are drastically reduced.

But what truly sets decentralized credit bureaus apart is their portability and sovereignty. In today's system, your creditworthiness exists in silos. If your credit history is compiled by one bureau and you move across borders or even change lenders, your data may not follow you. You have limited control over it. You often can't see what's been recorded in real time, nor challenge inaccuracies without a bureaucratic fight. In a decentralized model, the borrower owns their data. The ledger is public or semi-public, but access to specific data points is controlled via private keys. This empowers individuals and businesses to carry their credit reputation with them anywhere in the world, independent of institutions.

Decentralized credit systems are already taking shape. Projects like Bloom, Wala, and Akros are experimenting with blockchain-based credit scoring that builds a borrower profile from multiple sources: transaction history, mobile payments, utility bills, peer endorsements, and smart contract performance. In many of these systems, users begin to build credit by staking tokens, repaying microloans, or completing identity verifications via biometric or decentralized ID protocols. The behavior is recorded transparently and becomes part of a distributed reputation network. Instead of waiting for a bureau to compile and score them, users actively curate their financial identity.

This shift is particularly important in emerging markets, where formal credit infrastructures are underdeveloped or inaccessible to large portions of the population. In Sub-Saharan Africa, Southeast Asia, and parts of Latin America, blockchain-based lending platforms are offering alternatives that don't rely on Western-style credit bureaus. A farmer in Kenya can access a microloan based on mobile phone data and repayment history from a blockchain-verified savings group. A street vendor in Manila can establish a credit history by repaying solar panel installments logged on-chain. These systems don't ask, "What is your score?" They ask, "What does the ledger say you've done?"

This trustless, transparent approach has advantages beyond access. It also enhances security and reduces fraud. Centralized databases are prime targets for hackers. When Equifax was breached in 2017, the personal data of 147 million Americans was exposed—including names, birthdates, addresses, and Social Security numbers. In a decentralized system, there is no single point of failure. Even if one node is compromised, the data remains secure across the network. And because blockchain records are time-stamped and cryptographically verified, any attempt at manipulation is immediately evident.

Of course, decentralized credit systems come with their own challenges. The first is standardization. In a global system of peer-to-peer credit verification, how do we ensure consistency in data formats, scoring logic, and trustworthiness of inputs? Different blockchain protocols may interpret risk differently. A network that relies heavily on crypto transaction history may not accurately capture the operational nuances of a traditional small business. Bridging these gaps will require interoperability protocols and collaborative standards across platforms.

Another challenge is privacy. Blockchain is, by design, transparent. Every transaction is recorded and, depending on the chain, visible to anyone with access. This creates tension when dealing with sensitive financial data. Solutions like zero-knowledge proofs and privacy-preserving smart contracts are emerging to address this concern—allowing verification without revealing the underlying data—but these tools are still maturing. Ensuring that a borrower's data is secure, private, and compliant with global data protection laws will be critical to widespread adoption.

Moreover, there is the issue of adoption itself. Credit bureaus, banks, and regulators are deeply entrenched in the current system. Moving toward decentralization isn't just a technological shift—it's a cultural and institutional one. It means rethinking risk, redistributing power, and trusting in code rather than corporations. That's a difficult leap for many, especially in jurisdictions where blockchain technology remains misunderstood or politically controversial. Yet, forward-looking institutions are beginning to explore hybrid models—where traditional credit reporting coexists with blockchain-backed verification systems, gradually merging the best of both worlds.

Smart contracts play a vital role in enabling this vision. They allow for programmable lending agreements that execute automatically when predefined conditions are met. A business that takes out a working capital loan on a decentralized platform can have the terms encoded directly into the smart contract: interest rate, repayment schedule, collateral requirements, and default consequences. As payments are made, the contract updates the borrower's on-chain reputation. No manual reporting is required. No third-party validation is needed. The ledger becomes a living record of accountability.

For lenders, this reduces operational overhead and risk. They no longer need to rely on unverifiable claims or static credit reports. They can assess a borrower's reputation directly from the blockchain. Did the borrower repay their last five loans on time? Did they default on a contract two years ago? Are they actively transacting or sitting idle? The answers are immutable, time-stamped, and available without a phone call or a faxed statement.

For borrowers, especially small businesses, this is transformative. They can bypass traditional gatekeepers, build a reputation based on real-world behavior, and access credit globally—sometimes with lower fees, fewer delays, and more favorable terms. In effect, they become sovereign financial actors, leveraging a transparent, decentralized infrastructure to grow on their own terms.

But perhaps the most radical promise of decentralized credit bureaus is philosophical: they reimagine trust not as something bestowed by authority, but as something earned through action and encoded in public memory. In this system, no one grants creditworthiness—it is proven. There is no central bureau to correct, appeal to, or depend on. The record speaks for itself, and all actors are bound by the same immutable ledger.

As we move deeper into this new financial era, the role of blockchain in credit reporting will only grow. It will force institutions to re-examine their assumptions about risk, transparency, and data ownership. It will challenge policymakers to write new frameworks for a world where trust is not delegated, but distributed. And it will empower borrowers—especially those historically excluded from the credit system—to assert their presence, prove their reliability, and access the capital they need to thrive.

The age of centralized credit bureaus is waning. In its place, a new architecture is emerging—one where every transaction is a vote of confidence, every repayment is a digital testament, and every participant becomes a co-author of their financial story. Trust, in this world, is not asked for. It is demonstrated, recorded, and cryptographically secured. The revolution will not be scored. It will be verified.

3.2 Cross-Border Credit Portability

The concept of credit has always been tightly linked to geography. A business's creditworthiness, traditionally speaking, was bounded by jurisdiction—by the national laws, banking regulations, and domestic credit reporting agencies that governed its operations. A company might have an impeccable track record in its home country, with years of responsible borrowing and repayment, yet find itself treated like a blank slate—or worse, a risk—once it sought capital beyond its borders. For decades, this territorial rigidity was seen as an unfortunate reality of doing business internationally. But blockchain is now dismantling that constraint, introducing a new era of credit portability that transcends borders and local biases.

Cross-border credit portability refers to the ability of a business to carry its credit profile from one region to another without needing to reestablish a financial reputation from scratch. It's a simple idea with transformative implications. In the legacy system, credit records are stored in centralized databases maintained by national bureaus. These databases are often siloed and incompatible with each other, governed by different rules, formats, and privacy standards. As a result, when a business expands internationally—whether setting up a subsidiary, entering a new supply chain, or seeking foreign investment—it is often forced to rebuild its credit identity from the ground up. The time, cost, and bureaucratic inertia involved in that process not only stifles opportunity but punishes entrepreneurial ambition.

Blockchain technology changes this paradigm by enabling the creation of universally accessible, tamper-proof credit histories that can be viewed and verified anywhere in the world. Because data on the blockchain is decentralized, it exists outside of national jurisdictional control. Once a credit transaction is recorded—whether a loan repayment, a smart contract fulfillment, or a verified identity credential—it becomes part of a permanent, global record. This record can be accessed by lenders across continents, allowing them to evaluate borrowers based on actual historical behavior, rather than geographic assumptions or missing documentation.

For small and medium-sized enterprises (SMEs), the implications are enormous. An exporter in Vietnam that has built a solid repayment track record with a local microfinance platform using blockchain-based systems can use that same record to access credit from a logistics firm in Germany or an investment fund in Singapore. The borrower doesn't need to translate financial statements or go through months of application processes. The blockchain ledger tells the story—instantaneously and credibly. Trust, once limited to local ecosystems, becomes global.

In developing regions, where traditional credit bureaus are weak or nonexistent, cross-border credit portability can open entirely new financial pathways. Entrepreneurs who work across informal economies often lack formal proof of credit history. They may use mobile money platforms, barter systems, or peer-lending circles that never report to central authorities. But when those transactions are logged on a blockchain—whether through DeFi protocols, decentralized microloans, or token-based escrow systems—they create a data trail. That trail becomes the foundation of a portable financial identity, one that can travel with the borrower wherever they go.

This mobility also benefits lenders and investors. Institutions looking to expand their portfolios into high-growth emerging markets no longer need to rely solely on local partners or limited third-party data. They can directly verify borrower performance, track repayment timelines, and assess behavioral reliability using blockchain analytics. This reduces information asymmetry—the biggest obstacle to cross-border lending—and enables risk-based pricing that reflects actual borrower quality rather than geopolitical stereotypes.

Yet credit portability is not just a question of access—it's also a question of interoperability. Different blockchain networks, DeFi platforms, and identity protocols don't always speak the same language. For true credit portability to work, the industry must move toward standardization and interoperability frameworks. This includes shared schemas for credit events, cross-chain communication tools, and decentralized identity (DID) systems that allow individuals and businesses to authenticate themselves in a consistent way across platforms.

Fortunately, progress is underway. Projects like the Decentralized Identity Foundation and the World Wide Web Consortium's DID specifications are working to define these standards. On the financial side, protocols such as Chainlink's Cross-Chain Interoperability Protocol (CCIP) are beginning to enable value and data transfer between blockchain networks. The convergence of these efforts points to a future where credit is no longer locked into nation-states, but flows freely and securely through global digital infrastructures.

There are still regulatory hurdles to consider. Different countries have different laws governing data privacy, credit reporting, and financial inclusion. A blockchain-based credit profile that is fully transparent might violate privacy rules in one jurisdiction even while being standard practice in another. Cross-border compliance will require a delicate balance between transparency and data sovereignty. Privacy-preserving technologies—such as zero-knowledge proofs, selective disclosure protocols, and encrypted credentials—will play a critical role in this balancing act, allowing verifiable credit information to be shared without exposing sensitive personal or commercial data.

As blockchain-based credit systems mature, it's likely that we'll see the rise of credit "passports"—self-sovereign digital profiles that businesses can carry with them from one financial relationship to another. These passports won't be issued by governments or bureaus, but generated through the aggregation of verified activity: completed contracts, repaid loans, earned reputations. Like a well-reviewed seller on a marketplace, a business's blockchain credit identity will become a portable badge of trust.

In this emerging system, access to capital is no longer a function of where you are, but how you've behaved—and that's a radically more inclusive vision of finance. By removing the artificial walls erected by geography, blockchain offers a world where trust

41

follows the individual or the business, not the institution. It's a future where credit history is as mobile as the entrepreneur, as borderless as the internet, and as decentralized as the blockchain itself.

3.3 Programmable Credit: Smart Contract Lending

While blockchain technology offers transparency and decentralization, it is the introduction of smart contracts that unlocks its most disruptive financial potential. Smart contracts are self-executing agreements written in code, stored on the blockchain, and triggered automatically when predefined conditions are met. In the realm of credit, this means that loan agreements, repayment schedules, collateral management, and even default protocols can be programmed directly into the logic of the contract itself. This marks a revolutionary departure from traditional lending systems, which rely on human intermediaries, paperwork, and institutional enforcement to manage credit relationships.

Programmable credit shifts lending from a process governed by negotiation and oversight to one governed by code. The contract no longer needs to be interpreted, enforced, or mediated. It simply runs, autonomously and deterministically, based on the logic agreed upon by both parties. This not only reduces friction and cost but eliminates ambiguity. There are no disputes about what the terms mean, because the terms are literal, executed exactly as written.

Consider a simple example. A decentralized platform facilitates a business loan to a small artisan in Peru. The smart contract stipulates that repayments are to be made weekly, with a specific token deducted from the borrower's digital wallet. If a repayment is late, a grace period is activated. If payment still isn't made, a secondary clause triggers collateral lock-up. The lender doesn't need to call, email, or send a notice. The contract enforces itself. The artisan doesn't need to navigate legal threats or bank bureaucracy—the terms were known in advance, and the consequences are automatic.

This automation is particularly powerful for peer-to-peer lending, invoice factoring, and microfinance. A freelancer in Ghana can borrow against a pending invoice logged on-chain. The smart contract is programmed to release funds upon delivery confirmation, and repayment is deducted when the invoice is settled. No middlemen, no chasing, no late fees imposed at someone's discretion. Just logic, executed reliably.

But programmable credit goes beyond enforcement—it also enables creativity. Lenders can design loans with dynamic terms that adjust based on real-time conditions. For instance, a merchant cash advance could be structured to draw repayments as a percentage of daily sales, with the smart contract linked directly to a point-of-sale system. If business is slow, the repayment is smaller. If sales spike, the repayment increases. This model reduces pressure on the borrower and aligns lender incentives with borrower success.

Smart contracts also enable credit to be composable. In decentralized finance, lending products can be integrated with other services—insurance, staking, yield farming—into modular, interoperable systems. A small business could take out a loan whose interest payments are automatically offset by staking returns from idle capital, or whose collateral is insured via an external protocol. This level of financial engineering is simply not feasible in traditional finance, where each service is siloed and requires manual coordination.

One of the most compelling aspects of programmable credit is transparency. All transactions, repayments, defaults, and term changes are recorded on-chain. Lenders and regulators can audit histories instantly. Borrowers can verify that terms haven't changed or been manipulated. This eliminates many of the trust issues that plague conventional credit systems, especially in regions where contract enforcement is weak or legal systems are slow.

Still, programmable credit comes with its own set of complexities. Writing smart contracts requires technical expertise, and errors in code can be costly. A bug in a contract's logic could lock funds indefinitely or trigger unintended consequences. This risk has prompted the emergence of auditing firms that specialize in reviewing smart contracts for security and correctness. As the ecosystem matures, more user-friendly platforms are emerging—no-code or low-code environments that allow lenders and borrowers to customize loan agreements without needing to write Solidity or Rust.

Regulatory compliance is also a live question. Programmable credit challenges traditional notions of liability, jurisdiction, and consumer protection. If a borrower defaults and a contract automatically seizes collateral, is there a right to appeal? What happens if the terms violate local lending laws? In a decentralized context, who is legally responsible—the platform, the developer, the borrower? These questions are far from resolved, and they point to the need for legal frameworks that can accommodate autonomous finance while preserving fundamental rights.

Despite these challenges, the promise of programmable credit is immense. It creates a world where lending is not only decentralized but intelligent—able to adapt to context, respond to data, and execute complex financial logic without friction. It reduces cost, increases access, and builds systems that scale with minimal human intervention. It also democratizes financial innovation. A developer in Nairobi can build a new lending protocol and deploy it globally in days. An entrepreneur in Istanbul can borrow from a decentralized fund without ever speaking to a banker. A cooperative in Argentina can manage shared credit through a community-governed smart contract that reflects their values, not a foreign institution's policies.

In short, programmable credit takes the core idea of lending—trust, agreement, obligation—and reimagines it for the decentralized age. No longer reliant on paper, signatures, or personal connections, credit becomes a service governed by logic, powered by networks, and accessible to anyone with a wallet and a signal. The old system asked you to prove yourself, apply, and wait. The new system sees what you've done, encodes it, and responds—immediately and precisely.

As we look ahead, the rise of smart contract lending signals more than just a change in tools. It reflects a deeper philosophical shift: from reliance on institutions to reliance on protocols, from human discretion to algorithmic fairness, from centralized permission to decentralized access. Programmable credit is not just efficient. It is transformative. And its full potential is only just beginning to unfold.

Chapter 4: Open Banking and API-Driven Credit Decisions

4.1 Real-Time Financial Data Integration

The world of financial services has always depended on data. For generations, the problem wasn't that data didn't exist—it was that it was scattered, locked behind institutional walls, outdated by the time it was accessed, or available only to those with the right connections or insider access. Businesses seeking credit were routinely asked to provide documentation weeks or months old. Lenders, in turn, made decisions based on spreadsheets, PDFs, tax returns, and static bank statements. This process, while familiar, was riddled with blind spots. It lacked the precision, timeliness, and depth needed to assess the dynamic realities of modern business operations. And yet, for years, it was considered the best available method.

That is no longer the case.

Open banking has changed the game entirely. Enabled by legislation in many parts of the world—like the Revised Payment Services Directive (PSD2) in Europe and similar frameworks elsewhere—open banking mandates that banks must allow third-party access to customer data when authorized by the customer. What began as a regulatory push for transparency and competition has now blossomed into one of the most significant transformations in the history of finance. Combined with the power of APIs (Application Programming Interfaces), open banking has unlocked real-time financial data integration on a scale that was unthinkable just a decade ago.

For credit decisioning, this is revolutionary.

Imagine a lender evaluating a business loan application. In the traditional model, the underwriter would receive a balance sheet from six months ago, a couple of scanned invoices, and maybe a tax return from the previous fiscal year. That information would be combined with a credit score—often tied to the business owner's personal finances—and used to generate a lending decision that might affect the business for years. Every part of that process is rooted in the past. None of it accounts for what's happening today or how the business is performing right now.

With open banking and API access, that same lender can, with the borrower's consent, plug directly into the business's bank account, accounting software, and revenue platforms in real time. They can see current cash flow, verify deposits from key clients, monitor seasonality, detect payroll events, and even review expense categories. They no longer have to guess whether the business is healthy—they can observe it.

Real-time data integration doesn't just reduce friction; it fundamentally improves risk assessment. Lenders can identify early warning signs of distress—like shrinking margins, delayed payments to suppliers, or unexpected drops in revenue—weeks or months before a missed payment would traditionally raise alarm bells. On the other side, they can also detect indicators of growth, such as increasing customer acquisition, expanding payroll, or higher recurring revenue. Credit offers can then be adjusted accordingly, becoming more responsive, personalized, and supportive.

This dynamic responsiveness has led to the emergence of real-time underwriting—credit decisions that are no longer made once and forgotten but updated continuously as new data becomes available. A business approved for a $50,000 line of credit might see that limit increase to $70,000 after a few months of strong cash flow and customer growth. Conversely, the same system can trigger a review or reduction in exposure if the data suggests a downturn is unfolding. This adaptive model helps manage risk far more effectively than reactive processes ever could.

One of the most transformative outcomes of real-time data integration is its impact on credit access for businesses traditionally excluded from the system. Startups, for instance, often struggle to secure credit because they lack long-term financial histories. Yet they may have active customers, growing recurring revenue, and healthy profit margins—none of which are captured by standard credit scoring models. By tapping into APIs from platforms like Stripe, Shopify, QuickBooks, or Xero, lenders can now evaluate these businesses on the basis of their actual activity, not their age or lack of collateral.

In the gig economy, where businesses are increasingly fragmented and fluid, this kind of integration is essential. A freelancer managing multiple income streams across platforms like Upwork, PayPal, and Revolut can aggregate their income history through open banking APIs, creating a verifiable, unified record of earnings that supports their creditworthiness. This allows lenders to serve a demographic that was previously invisible to the traditional banking system—not because it wasn't trustworthy, but because the tools to see it didn't exist.

The integration of real-time financial data also creates new opportunities for embedded finance. Software providers—such as ecommerce platforms, ERP systems, or payment processors—can now offer lending products directly within their user interfaces, based on live data from their own ecosystems. This means that a business using a payroll platform might be pre-approved for a short-term loan based on its real-time cash reserves and payroll obligations. The decision happens behind the scenes, and the offer appears contextually—perhaps just when the user is processing payroll and notices a cash shortfall.

This kind of credit experience—fast, context-aware, and personalized—would be impossible without the granular visibility that APIs and open banking provide. It also benefits from automation. Rules can be set in advance, and credit models can be refined in real time. For example, a lender might automatically pre-approve businesses that meet certain revenue consistency and expense ratio thresholds, or flag those whose accounts show early signs of financial distress. These systems can scale across thousands or millions of users without manual review, dramatically reducing operational costs while improving service quality.

Transparency is another major advantage. Borrowers can be shown exactly which data points are being used to evaluate their applications, creating a more informed and empowered customer. Instead of being told "you didn't qualify," they can see that revenue dipped below a key threshold or that outstanding invoices have remained unpaid for too long. This kind of clarity invites collaboration and behavior change, turning the credit process into a dialogue rather than a verdict.

For lenders, this transparency also improves compliance. Real-time access to validated data reduces the risk of fraud and document manipulation, a common concern in traditional loan applications. With API connections, there's no need to rely on PDFs or scanned documents that can be doctored. The data comes directly from the source, authenticated and timestamped, reducing reliance on assumptions or guesswork.

Open banking also supports financial inclusion in new ways. In many parts of the world, businesses operate in cash-heavy environments or informal sectors, making it difficult for them to build formal credit profiles. However, with the rise of mobile banking, digital wallets, and alternative payment rails, many of these businesses are now transacting digitally—just not within traditional bank accounts. Through API integrations with these platforms, their financial activity can now be captured, analyzed, and used as the basis for credit decisions. This makes it possible to serve a broader swath of the global economy with relevant, appropriately priced lending products.

Despite its promise, real-time data integration does come with challenges. Data quality varies across platforms, and not all integrations are created equal. A business may use multiple accounting systems or have inconsistencies in categorization that make comparison difficult. Moreover, real-time access requires robust consent frameworks and secure authentication protocols to ensure data is not abused or accessed without permission. These concerns have prompted the development of open banking standards that prioritize customer control, encryption, and traceability.

Lenders must also consider how to interpret the flood of real-time information. Having access to data is not the same as understanding it. That's where analytics and machine learning come into play. Risk engines must be designed not only to process the raw numbers, but to contextualize them. A sudden dip in cash flow might signal trouble in one business, while in another—perhaps a highly seasonal operation—it could be entirely normal. The ability to distinguish signal from noise is essential.

As open banking evolves, the ecosystem around it continues to expand. Third-party data aggregators, API management platforms, and fintech middleware are creating bridges between institutions and businesses, simplifying the integration process. Meanwhile, regulators are beginning to recognize the importance of portability and standardization. By requiring banks to provide consistent, structured access to financial data, governments are fostering competition, reducing monopolistic data practices, and enabling a new generation of lending models to thrive.

In many ways, real-time data integration represents the convergence of two long-standing goals in credit: greater accuracy and greater inclusivity. By seeing businesses as they are today—not as they were a year ago—lenders can make smarter decisions. By removing the barriers of static documentation and outdated scoring systems, they can serve more borrowers, more fairly. And by embedding these capabilities into the digital platforms that businesses already use, they can deliver credit experiences that are frictionless, intuitive, and aligned with the realities of the modern economy.

The old model of credit was built for a world of folders, bankers' hours, and quarterly reports. The new model is built for APIs, automation, and immediacy. Real-time financial data integration isn't just a technical upgrade—it's a redefinition of what credit means, how it's earned, and who gets to access it. As open banking continues to mature, it will lay the foundation for a financial system that is not only more efficient, but more equitable—one where credit follows the truth of data, not the shadows of history.

4.2 Automated Financial Statement Generation

The financial statement has long stood as the central document in the lender's toolkit—a seemingly straightforward report offering insight into the health of a business. Balance sheets, income statements, and cash flow reports have served as the foundation upon which credit decisions are built. Yet, while these documents are essential, the way they are generated and used in the credit process has remained stubbornly manual and retrospective.

Borrowers often scramble to produce them under tight deadlines, drawing on fragmented accounting systems, reconciling errors, and assembling spreadsheets that may or may not reflect real-time accuracy. For lenders, verifying these documents and ensuring their integrity becomes another slow and friction-filled step in an already cumbersome underwriting process. But as financial technology has evolved and open banking has made data more accessible, the next logical leap is unfolding: the automation of financial statement generation.

Automated financial statement generation represents a pivotal shift in how businesses communicate their financial story to external parties. Rather than producing statements manually, businesses can now connect their accounting software, bank feeds, payment processors, and other operational platforms to a centralized engine that constructs accurate, up-to-date financial statements automatically. These statements can be generated on demand, with real-time data reflecting the current position of the business—not where it stood at the end of last quarter or fiscal year.

This automation solves a core inefficiency that has plagued both borrowers and lenders for decades. For borrowers, preparing statements is often a time-consuming and error-prone task. Small businesses, in particular, may not have dedicated financial personnel or the expertise to create formal financial reports. Their records may be stored across disparate systems—some in cloud-based accounting software, others in spreadsheets, paper receipts, or legacy invoicing platforms. The need to manually reconcile this information introduces delays and often results in inaccuracies that undermine confidence in the borrower's reliability.

When financial statements are automated, this fragmented process disappears. Instead, once connected to the appropriate data sources, the system pulls in the relevant information, reconciles it using predefined logic, and formats it into standard financial statements that comply with generally accepted accounting principles (GAAP) or international standards, depending on the jurisdiction. These statements can be refreshed daily, weekly, or even hourly, ensuring that the financial picture is always current. This continuous availability of accurate financial data is a game-changer for credit providers.

For lenders, the benefits are equally profound. Automated statements provide a standardized, structured view of a borrower's financial health without the need for document verification, manual entry, or reconciliation. The risks of data tampering, fraud, or misrepresentation are significantly reduced, especially when the underlying data comes directly from bank feeds and verified systems. This means credit decisions can be made with greater speed and confidence. Lenders no longer need to ask, "Is this document trustworthy?" because the data chain from transaction to statement is fully traceable and auditable.

Beyond improving accuracy and reducing fraud, automation also enhances analytical power. Because the statements are generated digitally, they can be parsed, queried, and modeled instantly. Lenders can run simulations, stress-test financial assumptions, and benchmark performance against sector peers—all without requesting additional data from the borrower. This level of financial visibility was once reserved for large enterprises with full-time financial reporting teams. Now, it's becoming accessible to small and medium-sized businesses through the power of automation.

There is also a broader democratizing effect at play. In many regions of the world, small businesses lack formal documentation not because they are untrustworthy or informal, but because the costs of compliance are too high. Hiring accountants, retaining bookkeepers, and producing monthly reports can be prohibitively expensive. By automating financial statement generation, these businesses can suddenly participate in formal credit markets with minimal additional effort. They no longer need to guess at what a lender wants to see—they can generate and share the exact documents required with a few clicks.

Moreover, these automated systems are beginning to incorporate contextual intelligence. They don't just aggregate numbers— they understand the relationships between them. They can flag anomalies, suggest corrections, and even provide narrative explanations of what's driving changes in key metrics. A lender reviewing an income statement might see not just the revenue number but a generated summary explaining that a spike in sales was due to a holiday promotion, or that a dip in profit margins correlates with a temporary increase in supplier costs. These insights can be produced in natural language, making the data accessible even to non-financial stakeholders.

Of course, automation doesn't mean the removal of human oversight entirely. Financial professionals still play a role in reviewing statements, interpreting subtleties, and providing strategic guidance. But the mechanical work—the tedious reconciliation, formatting, and compiling of data—can now be offloaded to machines. This frees up time for higher-value work and accelerates the lending process for all parties involved.

Privacy and data security are central considerations in this new model. When businesses allow third parties to access their financial data, they must trust that the systems are secure and compliant with relevant regulations. Fortunately, many automated financial statement providers use encrypted data pipelines, secure authentication protocols, and audit logs to ensure transparency and protection. Additionally, businesses can typically control what data is shared, with whom, and for how long. This level of granular control helps build trust and encourages broader adoption.

The rise of API-based accounting integrations has played a crucial role in making automated statement generation viable. Platforms like QuickBooks, Xero, FreshBooks, and Wave now offer rich APIs that allow third-party systems to pull transaction-level data, categorize expenses, track invoices, and generate reports automatically. When combined with open banking data—such as live bank balances and transaction feeds—a comprehensive financial picture emerges that is both up-to-date and deeply informative.

As the ecosystem matures, we can expect to see further innovation in how financial statements are generated, interpreted, and used. Artificial intelligence will increasingly be layered on top of automated systems, offering predictive insights and scenario modeling. Businesses will be able to test how a change in revenue, cost of goods sold, or payroll expenses would impact their future cash flow and borrowing capacity. Lenders, in turn, will use these tools to build more nuanced risk models that go beyond historical averages and static ratios.

Ultimately, automated financial statement generation represents more than just a convenience—it is a structural shift in how businesses represent themselves and how lenders understand them. It replaces friction with fluidity, opacity with transparency, and delay with immediacy. In doing so, it lays the groundwork for a credit system that is not only more efficient but fundamentally more fair—where decisions are based on the truth of current financial behavior, not the paperwork of the past.

4.3 Embedded Lending in Business Software

The idea of borrowing money has traditionally been associated with distinct, formal steps: applying for a loan, submitting documentation, waiting for approval, and finally receiving the funds. It's a process that historically occurred outside of a business's day-to-day operations—something separate from their work, their systems, and their tools. But that model is now dissolving. A new paradigm is emerging in which credit is not just something applied for but something embedded—integrated directly into the software platforms businesses already use to manage their operations. This is the world of embedded lending, and it is fundamentally altering how, when, and why businesses access capital.

Embedded lending refers to the integration of credit products into non-financial business software, allowing users to access financing seamlessly within the tools they use to sell, manage, and grow their businesses. Rather than going to a bank or filling out a traditional loan application, a business owner may be offered a pre-approved credit line while managing their inventory, a short-term loan while issuing payroll, or invoice financing at the moment of generating a bill for a client. The offer appears contextually, within the platform itself, informed by real-time data, and tailored to the user's immediate needs.

This new form of lending is made possible by the confluence of open APIs, cloud software, and real-time financial data. Platforms that manage commerce, logistics, payroll, or accounting already have deep insights into a business's operations. They see sales trends, customer payment behavior, expenses, and cash flow patterns. When these platforms partner with embedded lenders, they can turn this information into risk profiles, enabling credit assessments without the user ever needing to leave the interface.

For the business owner, the experience is transformative. No paperwork, no credit score queries, no meetings. Just a message: "Based on your recent sales, you're eligible for $20,000 in working capital—click here to accept." The entire process, from offer to funding, can happen in minutes. Because the software already holds the necessary data—connected bank accounts, historical invoices, recurring expenses—there is no need for manual verification. Approval is based on the actual performance of the business, not on lagging indicators or outdated assumptions.

This embedded model also enhances timing. Credit is offered at the precise moment it is needed, reducing financial friction. A merchant on an ecommerce platform might receive an offer to finance their next inventory purchase after a successful sales campaign. A freelancer might be offered invoice factoring when their client payment is pending but delayed. A service-based business could access payroll loans when faced with a short-term cash crunch during seasonal slowdowns. Because the system knows the context, the offer can be not only timely but relevant—customized to the specific event unfolding in the business lifecycle.

Embedded lending is not a one-size-fits-all model. It can take many forms: lines of credit, term loans, revenue-based financing, pay-later options for B2B purchases, and more. The key innovation is not the structure of the loan itself, but its delivery. By bringing lending into the operational workflow, these systems blur the line between banking and business tools, creating a new category of "credit as a feature" rather than a separate service.

The result is a more intuitive, frictionless experience that aligns with how modern businesses operate. Just as embedded payments have made it possible to accept credit cards or digital wallets directly within apps, embedded lending makes credit available as a seamless extension of business activity. There's no need to switch platforms, duplicate data entry, or explain your business to a stranger. The software already knows who you are.

For lenders, this model reduces customer acquisition costs and increases data quality. Rather than relying on self-reported financials, they gain access to verified, real-time data from the source. Risk models can be updated continuously, and default risk is lowered due to better timing and contextual awareness. Moreover, repayment can be automated. For example, a loan made via a point-of-sale platform might be repaid automatically through a percentage of future transactions, reducing administrative overhead and improving collection rates.

However, embedded lending also introduces new responsibilities. Software providers must ensure transparency in the terms offered, avoid predatory structures, and provide clear customer support. Lenders, in turn, must navigate compliance requirements in a fragmented regulatory landscape, where embedded finance often operates in gray zones between banking and commerce. As the space grows, regulators are paying closer attention, and providers must prioritize consumer protection and ethical lending practices.

There are also strategic implications for businesses that build and use these systems. Software companies that offer embedded lending gain a competitive edge—they provide not just tools, but resources. Lenders that embrace embedded models can reach new markets and serve borrowers more efficiently. And businesses that tap into these systems gain faster, smarter access to capital—reducing barriers to growth, smoothing out cash flow volatility, and building resilience in uncertain times.

As embedded finance becomes more sophisticated, we'll see increased convergence between operational data and financial services. Loan offers will be powered not just by past behavior but by predictive insights. A business whose supply chain data suggests increased demand may be offered proactive financing for expansion. A contractor with rising client bookings may be eligible for early access to funds for hiring. In every case, the key is integration—lending that is not an afterthought, but a built-in function of doing business in a digital economy.

In sum, embedded lending is more than a trend. It is a structural transformation in the delivery of credit, making it more immediate, contextual, and accessible. It reduces barriers, improves timing, and ensures that capital flows where it is needed most—at the exact moment it can make the biggest difference. As this model spreads, it will redefine not only how credit is delivered, but how it is perceived: not as a favor granted by distant institutions, but as a native function of the software businesses already rely on. In this new model, the future of credit is not at the bank. It's in your software.

Chapter 5: Alternative Data Sources: Beyond Bank Statements

5.1 The Internet of Things (IoT) Credit Revolution

For much of modern financial history, credit decisions have been tethered to a narrow scope of data: bank statements, tax returns, credit scores, and financial ratios. These sources, while useful, have painted only part of the picture—often a delayed, incomplete, or distorted version of a business's actual operations. As the economy has become more digitized and interconnected, it has become increasingly evident that the traditional data points used for underwriting are inadequate for understanding the real-time vitality of an enterprise. Enter the Internet of Things (IoT)—a vast, decentralized network of connected devices silently collecting, transmitting, and analyzing physical-world data. While originally designed to optimize logistics, manufacturing, and consumer convenience, the IoT is now catalyzing a quiet revolution in credit: a transformation in how lenders understand, measure, and trust borrowers.

At the most basic level, IoT devices collect information from the physical environment. Sensors on factory equipment measure productivity and uptime. GPS-enabled devices track vehicle usage, delivery timelines, and asset location. Smart meters log energy consumption and efficiency. Cold chain monitors report temperature integrity for perishable goods. Inventory management systems track stock levels in real time. Each of these devices produces a continuous stream of data that, when properly interpreted, reveals an intimate portrait of how a business functions—not just how it claims to.

The implications of this are vast. In traditional lending, a manufacturer might submit a profit-and-loss statement showing quarterly revenue, net margins, and outstanding liabilities. But what that statement doesn't reveal is whether the company's machines are actually running consistently, whether downtime has increased, or whether product output has slowed due to faulty equipment. A lender evaluating that business based solely on financial statements might approve a loan that looks justified on paper but fails to detect brewing operational risk. With IoT data in the mix, the story becomes clearer. Real-time telemetry from production lines shows whether output is stable or declining. Maintenance logs, automatically generated by smart devices, indicate whether key machinery is being serviced regularly or nearing failure. In short, the physical health of the business becomes visible—and quantifiable.

IoT-based underwriting flips the credit conversation from retrospective to current and even predictive. It enables lenders to move beyond the numbers on a spreadsheet and into the daily rhythm of the business itself. For agricultural enterprises, this might mean accessing data from soil sensors, irrigation controls, drone surveys, and harvest monitors. A lender can see whether the farm is operating efficiently, how crops are developing, and whether environmental conditions are being properly managed— all without waiting for year-end results. For logistics companies, real-time fleet data reveals whether delivery targets are being met, fuel efficiency is improving, or routes are optimized. These insights help underwriters assess the borrower not just in terms of reported income but operational performance.

This shift is especially powerful in sectors traditionally underserved by the credit system. Many small businesses in transportation, agriculture, and light manufacturing operate in ways that are capital-intensive, geographically dispersed, and seasonally variable—factors that traditional financial models struggle to accommodate. But these same businesses are increasingly equipped with sensors, trackers, and digital tools that capture how they operate. An independent trucker, for example, might lack a formal business plan or long credit history, but telematics from their truck can show consistent mileage, route efficiency, on-time deliveries, and low maintenance issues. These operational patterns signal discipline, reliability, and performance—all key indicators of creditworthiness, even in the absence of formal documents.

What makes IoT data particularly attractive is that it is self-generating and tamper-resistant. Unlike self-reported financials or subjective credit narratives, IoT data comes directly from devices deployed in the field. This makes it difficult to forge or manipulate. A refrigeration unit in a warehouse doesn't lie about temperature fluctuations. A smart scale in a shipping bay doesn't exaggerate throughput. For lenders, this integrity reduces risk and increases confidence in the insights drawn from the data. It also opens the door to automated monitoring, where loans can be disbursed, adjusted, or flagged based on IoT-driven performance benchmarks. For instance, a financing agreement might stipulate that a borrower's production rate must stay above a certain level for the credit line to remain open. If sensors detect a sustained drop in output, the system can trigger an alert, freeze further disbursements, or offer restructuring—all without human intervention.

The real power of IoT in lending, however, lies in its predictive capabilities. Because the data is continuous and granular, it allows for modeling future outcomes with surprising accuracy. If a machine begins to overheat more frequently, it may be at risk of failure, which could disrupt operations and affect cash flow. If traffic congestion on delivery routes increases, fuel costs might spike and margins shrink. These signals, when captured early, can inform risk models long before financial trouble surfaces in the books. In this way, IoT transforms underwriting into an exercise not of hindsight but of foresight.

This predictive lens is particularly valuable in asset-based lending. Consider a construction firm seeking financing to purchase new equipment. Traditionally, the lender would evaluate the company's balance sheet, appraise existing equipment, and calculate leverage ratios. But with IoT integration, the lender can also assess how existing machinery is being used. Are the excavators running at capacity? Are they idle for long stretches? Are maintenance issues frequent or rare? This operational insight helps the lender understand whether new equipment is truly needed, how it will likely be used, and whether the firm has the operational maturity to manage additional assets. The same principle applies to fleets, warehouses, generators, or any other capital-intensive equipment that can be instrumented with sensors.

Of course, the adoption of IoT in credit brings new challenges. The first is integration. IoT devices often operate in siloed systems, with proprietary data formats and limited interoperability. For lenders to harness this data effectively, standardization and connectivity protocols must be in place. This is where emerging platforms that aggregate and normalize IoT data across industries play a critical role. These platforms act as intermediaries between the raw signals produced by devices and the analytical engines used by credit providers.

Another issue is data governance. While IoT data may be less sensitive than personal financial records, it still raises questions about ownership, access, and usage rights. Businesses must be assured that sharing operational data for credit purposes will not compromise their competitive position or privacy. Lenders, in turn, must commit to transparency, ethical usage, and compliance with emerging regulations around machine-generated data. The development of consent frameworks, data-sharing agreements, and privacy-preserving analytics will be essential to building trust in IoT-powered credit systems.

There is also the matter of interpretability. Raw IoT data is complex and highly contextual. A temperature reading or vibration alert means little in isolation—it must be interpreted within the framework of a specific business model, industry norm, and operational goal. This is where artificial intelligence and machine learning intersect with IoT. By training models on large datasets of sensor readings and known outcomes, lenders can identify patterns that correlate with risk or success. The more data that is collected, the more refined and sector-specific these models become.

We are already beginning to see early deployments of IoT-based credit in emerging economies. In India, for example, fintech firms are using sensor data from tractors and irrigation systems to assess farmer productivity and offer microloans. In Latin America, logistics startups are leveraging vehicle telemetry to create dynamic risk scores for transport companies. In Europe, asset financiers are linking equipment leasing terms to real-time usage data, allowing for usage-based repayment structures. These experiments are not just novel—they are reshaping what it means to be "creditworthy" in a world where physical operations are as measurable as financial ones.

In the long term, IoT data may become a fundamental layer of credit infrastructure. Just as open banking has turned financial institutions into data providers, the IoT is transforming the physical world into a continuous source of economic insight. Every machine that moves, every sensor that records, every device that transmits becomes part of a decentralized credit oracle—a real-time narrative of business performance that can inform, enable, and safeguard lending at unprecedented levels of granularity.

For businesses, this shift offers an opportunity to unlock capital by demonstrating reliability not through bureaucracy, but through behavior. For lenders, it opens up new markets, reduces asymmetry, and provides early-warning systems that allow for more responsive, intelligent credit strategies. For the financial ecosystem as a whole, the IoT credit revolution marks a transition from abstraction to visibility—from judging a business by its paperwork to seeing it through the lens of its actions.

What lies ahead is a new credit paradigm, one that looks not just at what a borrower claims to be, but at how they actually operate in the world—machine by machine, task by task, moment by moment. In this paradigm, the heartbeat of a business is not measured quarterly but continuously, and the future of credit is written not just in numbers, but in signals. The Internet of Things has already reshaped industries from logistics to agriculture to energy. Now it is coming for finance—not as a disruptor, but as an informant, a partner, and a powerful new source of truth.

5.2 Social and Digital Footprint Analysis

The architecture of modern credit evaluation has traditionally overlooked one of the most revealing dimensions of a business's identity: its presence in the digital world. As commerce, marketing, communication, and reputation have all migrated online, the digital footprint left by a business now contains volumes of information—dynamic, behavioral, and context-rich data points that offer lenders a deeper understanding of operational authenticity, market relevance, and brand resilience. In the analog era, creditworthiness was gauged by ledgers, bank balances, and tax filings. But in today's connected world, these elements only form a partial narrative. The rest is written in online behavior, customer engagement, review patterns, website performance, and even sentiment on social media.

Social and digital footprint analysis is quickly becoming a powerful tool in alternative credit evaluation. It involves the systematic review of a business's online presence—its website, reviews, customer interactions, content consistency, and visibility across platforms—to generate a picture of credibility and momentum. This layer of data, while once seen as soft or subjective, is now being algorithmically quantified and used to inform real-world lending decisions. And in many cases, it has proven more predictive of success and reliability than traditional indicators.

For instance, a small business may lack formal credit history or collateral but have a robust, consistent digital presence. It may operate a well-designed, frequently updated website, run active and positively received social media accounts, and show up regularly in local business directories and Google reviews. Its customers might mention it positively across various forums, and its engagement metrics—such as comment response time, order fulfillment ratings, and digital ad performance—might reflect a business that is attentive, agile, and reputable. From the perspective of a lender using legacy underwriting criteria, this business might be invisible or high risk. But through the lens of digital footprint analysis, it appears vibrant, responsive, and trustworthy.

This approach opens access to a new class of borrower—especially small and micro-businesses born in the digital age. A craftsman selling on Etsy, an educator delivering online courses, a digital marketing consultant operating globally from a home office—all may lack formal banking relationships, physical assets, or traditional business credit. Yet their online reputation, their responsiveness to customers, their social proof through reviews and endorsements, and their digital infrastructure speak volumes about their reliability. These signals, once dismissed as anecdotal or intangible, are now being processed through machine learning models that convert them into structured risk assessments.

The methodology behind this transformation is both technical and behavioral. On the technical side, crawlers and data aggregation tools scan public-facing data sources to compile a detailed map of a business's digital footprint. This includes domain authority scores, website metadata, social media engagement metrics, review velocity and content, and cross-platform consistency. The behavioral layer involves natural language processing tools that analyze tone, sentiment, and relevance of mentions across user-generated content. Does the business respond politely to complaints? Are reviews improving or declining over time? Are their posts informative or promotional? These factors help build a multidimensional view of operational culture—something traditional data simply cannot reveal.

From a risk modeling perspective, the benefit of social and digital footprint analysis lies in its dynamism. Unlike static financial reports or historical credit scores, a digital footprint evolves in real time. A sudden drop in engagement, an influx of negative reviews, or the disappearance of previously active social media channels may signal operational instability. On the other hand, a spike in brand mentions, increased traffic to the website, or viral visibility may indicate growth potential or successful marketing campaigns. For lenders and investors, these trends offer early signals—green flags or red—that precede financial movement.

This is particularly useful in times of crisis or rapid economic change. During the pandemic, for example, many traditional risk metrics became unreliable as revenue collapsed, supply chains were disrupted, and borrowing patterns shifted. However, businesses with strong digital communities, high customer goodwill, and adaptive online strategies often weathered the storm better than expected. Their social engagement didn't vanish; their audiences stayed. They pivoted to new offerings, rebranded, launched campaigns, and communicated effectively—actions that were visible through their digital presence long before they showed up in profit and loss statements.

Still, integrating digital footprints into credit models requires careful calibration. Not all data is equally meaningful, and noise can distort the signal. A business might have many followers but no conversions. Reviews can be manipulated. Engagement can be purchased. This is where advanced algorithms come into play—filtering for authenticity, identifying fake or bot-driven content, and weighting data based on historical reliability. The goal is not to replace traditional risk metrics but to augment them with a dimension that captures the texture of business reality in the digital age.

In markets with low formal financial inclusion but high mobile and internet penetration, digital footprint analysis provides a critical bridge. Businesses that operate primarily through Facebook shops, WhatsApp groups, or Instagram storefronts often lack bank records but have thriving customer bases and strong reputational momentum. With the right tools, these patterns can be harnessed to create new models of trust, enabling lenders to reach borrowers that were previously out of scope.

The challenge is not only technical but also cultural. Financial institutions accustomed to black-and-white credit models must adjust to a world where shades of digital grey carry meaning. Credit officers need to be trained to interpret these new signals, platforms must develop interfaces that translate digital data into actionable insight, and regulatory frameworks will need to evolve to define what constitutes fair and explainable use of online behavioral data in credit decisions.

What emerges from this convergence is a more human portrait of the borrower—one that includes their digital voice, their public behavior, and their relevance in a connected marketplace. It is not a perfect system, nor is it immune to misuse, but it is far closer to how value is perceived, created, and measured in today's economy. By capturing how a business shows up in the digital world, social and digital footprint analysis helps lenders understand who the borrower is, how they operate, and why they matter—insights that are essential for making informed, inclusive, and resilient credit decisions in the 21st century.

5.3 Supply Chain and Partnership Intelligence

Creditworthiness, at its core, is about trust. Can a business be relied upon to fulfill its obligations, manage its resources, and sustain its operations over time? While traditional credit models have sought to answer this question by focusing on internal factors—balance sheets, revenue consistency, and repayment history—they often ignore the wider ecosystem in which a business operates. That ecosystem, however, is critical. A business is not an island. Its health is deeply connected to the stability, reliability, and behavior of its partners, suppliers, clients, and vendors. In a world of complex global trade, just-in-time delivery models, and intricate service networks, a business's success or failure often hinges as much on its relationships as on its books. This is where supply chain and partnership intelligence enters the conversation.

Supply chain and partnership intelligence refers to the integration of external network data—such as vendor reliability, customer concentration, logistics performance, and upstream dependency—into credit decisioning. Instead of viewing a business as a self-contained entity, lenders begin to assess it as part of a larger web. They look not only at what the business owns and earns, but at whom it relies on, how resilient those relationships are, and what risks or advantages stem from those connections.

This approach is particularly relevant in industries where supply chain volatility has become the norm. Over the past few years, disruptions triggered by pandemics, geopolitical conflict, natural disasters, and trade restrictions have exposed how fragile many supply chains really are. Businesses that appeared strong on paper found themselves unable to deliver products or fulfill services due to failures in their vendor base. Others, whose own operations were lean but whose partners were diversified, adaptive, and digitally connected, showed surprising resilience. In such cases, it was not the internal metrics alone but the strength of the external network that determined outcomes.

Incorporating partnership intelligence into credit models involves evaluating key components of the borrower's supply chain. This includes the diversification of suppliers, the financial health of key vendors, the presence of long-term contracts, and the quality of fulfillment performance. A business that relies heavily on a single supplier, especially in a high-risk jurisdiction or volatile industry, may carry higher credit risk. Conversely, a business with a broad, diversified vendor base, digitally tracked inventory, and backup fulfillment strategies demonstrates operational maturity and lower vulnerability to shocks.

Digitalization has made this analysis possible. Increasingly, businesses use supply chain management software that integrates with logistics providers, warehousing systems, inventory platforms, and procurement tools. These systems track order volumes, fulfillment timelines, backorder rates, and inventory turnover in real time. Lenders, through consented API access, can tap into this data to understand how goods flow through the business, how responsive it is to customer demand, and how robust its upstream relationships are.

Customer-side intelligence is equally important. A business may have a significant portion of its revenue concentrated in one or two clients. If those clients delay payments, change suppliers, or default, the impact can be catastrophic. Evaluating customer concentration risk, payment reliability, and contractual structures provides crucial context. A business with diversified revenue sources and long-standing customer relationships is inherently more stable than one dependent on a single flagship account, regardless of its revenue scale.

In service sectors, partnership intelligence takes on different forms. For a software firm, this might mean evaluating integration partners, white-label relationships, or platform dependencies. For a marketing agency, it could involve assessing referral networks, subcontractors, or content distribution agreements. The key insight remains the same: who does the business rely on to deliver what it promises?

This network-based approach to credit also enables collaborative risk mitigation. A lender may identify that a borrower's key supplier is experiencing delays or distress. Rather than waiting for the borrower to miss payments, the lender can intervene— perhaps offering bridge financing, restructuring timelines, or even supporting the borrower in sourcing alternatives. In this way, supply chain intelligence transforms credit from a binary approval mechanism into a living relationship informed by environmental signals.

Such strategies are already being piloted in trade finance and export credit. Firms like Tradeshift, Taulia, and C2FO analyze procurement data and invoice workflows to extend working capital solutions based on the behavior of buyers and suppliers, not just the financials of the borrower. In emerging markets, platforms are using mobile logistics data to assess the delivery performance of local vendors, enabling microcredit with higher reliability.

Partnership intelligence also supports sustainability and ESG-aligned lending. By analyzing the environmental and labor practices of suppliers, lenders can offer favorable terms to borrowers who work with responsible partners. This rewards ethical behavior, reduces long-term reputational risk, and supports compliance with increasingly stringent disclosure requirements in global trade.

Despite its promise, this model requires trust, standardization, and shared incentives. Businesses must be willing to share supply chain data, which may include competitive insights. Lenders must respect confidentiality and use the data only for agreed purposes. Platforms and standards must ensure interoperability so that data from various tools can be integrated seamlessly.

When done right, supply chain and partnership intelligence provides lenders with a 360-degree view of the business—one that includes not just what the business claims or owns, but how it behaves in relation to its partners, what it depends on, and how it adapts under pressure. This approach shifts the understanding of creditworthiness from static risk to systemic resilience. It recognizes that a business is only as strong as the network it relies on, and that credit decisions are best made not in isolation, but in full view of the business ecosystem.

In this light, the future of credit is not just about analyzing data—it's about understanding interdependence. By peering into the flows of supply, the patterns of partnership, and the webs of collaboration that define today's enterprises, lenders can make decisions that are not only more accurate, but also more aligned with the true complexity of the businesses they aim to serve.

Chapter 6: Instant Credit Decisions: The Need for Speed

6.1 Millisecond Decision Architecture

In the modern economy, speed is not a luxury—it is a necessity. Customers expect real-time responses, payments clear in seconds, and digital transactions settle with a single click. Credit, too, has entered this domain of immediacy. The days of waiting days or even weeks for a loan officer to review an application, verify documents, and return with a decision are quickly becoming a relic of the past. In their place emerges a new paradigm: instant credit decisions powered by a high-speed technological backbone that can assess, verify, and decide within milliseconds. This evolution, driven by data availability, advanced computing, and machine intelligence, is not just a matter of convenience. It's becoming the backbone of competitive financial infrastructure, especially for lenders operating in digital-first environments.

At the heart of this shift lies what can be described as millisecond decision architecture—a system design philosophy that allows credit evaluation, scoring, and approval to happen so quickly that the user perceives it as instantaneous. While to the borrower it appears simple—a single click leading to immediate approval or denial—behind the scenes is a sophisticated orchestration of data ingestion, risk modeling, identity verification, fraud detection, and compliance checks all occurring simultaneously. The complexity is hidden under layers of intelligent automation, high-performance computing, and deeply integrated data flows.

To appreciate the speed of these decisions, one must understand what is being processed. In traditional underwriting, a credit officer might manually assess an applicant's income statements, tax returns, collateral value, credit score, and business plan. This review could take hours per file, often longer when discrepancies arise. In contrast, a millisecond credit system pulls real-time data from APIs connected to the applicant's bank account, accounting software, transaction history, public registries, and even behavioral data from their digital activity. These systems synthesize hundreds, sometimes thousands, of data points, analyze them with pre-trained algorithms, check them against regulatory criteria, and return a risk score with accompanying decision logic—all within a fraction of a second.

This level of speed and accuracy demands a particular kind of system architecture. It is not enough to have fast computers or good algorithms. The entire process must be designed to minimize latency, reduce friction, and execute parallel processes efficiently. That begins with event-driven design. Rather than waiting for manual input, the system reacts to events in real time—data updates, customer actions, third-party inputs. Every interaction becomes a trigger for analysis. For example, the moment a business connects its accounting software, the system begins parsing financial data, evaluating cash flows, and detecting trends. The moment a digital signature is submitted, identity verification protocols begin scanning public records and anti-fraud databases.

To function at this velocity, data storage must be both vast and instantly accessible. Many lenders now rely on distributed databases, memory-first architectures, and streaming analytics platforms. Instead of retrieving data from disk, which takes time, they keep frequently accessed data in high-speed memory caches. Data lakes fed by open banking APIs, transaction logs, and third-party sources are constantly updated and indexed for rapid access. The system knows where to look, what to ignore, and how to prioritize information under tight computational deadlines.

Machine learning models, already trained on millions of past credit decisions, sit at the core of the scoring engine. These models do not operate in isolation—they are deployed within scalable environments that support concurrent processing. Thousands of applications can be evaluated at once, each fed through a flow that includes risk scoring, scenario testing, outcome simulation, and optimization of terms. Some models estimate default probability; others simulate cash flow resilience under stress. Some evaluate behavioral consistency, while others match applicants to the optimal loan product based on current market conditions.

To meet regulatory and security standards, identity verification and compliance checks must be equally rapid. Traditional Know Your Customer (KYC) and Anti-Money Laundering (AML) processes that once required physical documentation are now handled via automated scans, biometric verification, and third-party data services. An applicant's identity can be verified through a combination of government ID recognition, geolocation data, and facial recognition in under a second. Fraud detection engines, fueled by anomaly detection algorithms, cross-check the applicant's behavior against known fraud patterns, device fingerprints, and geospatial inconsistencies. These checks happen concurrently with risk modeling, not sequentially, reducing delay without compromising due diligence.

What makes millisecond decisioning possible is the use of decision orchestration layers. These are logic-based systems that determine, in real time, which models to apply, what data to retrieve, and which rules to enforce based on the specific context of the application. A different path may be taken for a first-time borrower versus a returning customer, or for a business in retail versus one in manufacturing. The orchestration engine ensures that each application is evaluated through a decision tree optimized for speed, accuracy, and relevance.

This type of architecture is particularly valuable in embedded lending environments, where credit is offered directly within software workflows—on ecommerce platforms, point-of-sale systems, payroll apps, or supply chain portals. In these contexts, speed is essential. The borrower is not sitting in a bank office waiting for a loan officer. They are checking out an inventory purchase, issuing an invoice, or managing payroll when the loan offer is made. If the credit decision is not immediate, the opportunity is lost. Millisecond processing allows the offer to appear instantly, contextually, and with full underwriting already completed in the background.

Another advantage of this architecture is continuous learning. Every application processed feeds back into the system, updating model weights, recalibrating risk thresholds, and refining decision paths. This feedback loop ensures that the system evolves, adapting to shifts in borrower behavior, macroeconomic conditions, and fraud tactics. The more the system processes, the smarter and faster it becomes. It moves beyond being a fixed set of rules into a living organism capable of adjusting in real time.

The human role in millisecond credit environments is not eliminated—it is redefined. Credit analysts no longer spend their time reviewing basic applications but instead focus on edge cases, policy development, and ethical oversight. Compliance teams no longer manually review every transaction but monitor model behavior, investigate flagged anomalies, and test for bias. Customer support shifts from explaining delays to guiding borrowers through opportunities surfaced by intelligent systems.

There are, of course, risks to this kind of velocity. Decisions made in milliseconds can propagate errors just as quickly if the underlying data or models are flawed. An incorrect rule, a biased algorithm, or a false signal can impact thousands of borrowers in seconds. That's why rigorous testing, real-time monitoring, and explainable AI tools are essential components of any millisecond decision system. Institutions must be able to explain every decision made by the system, not just to regulators, but to the borrowers themselves. Transparency must match speed.

Moreover, speed should not come at the expense of inclusion. Fast systems tend to favor borrowers with rich, structured, and digital data trails. Those operating outside the formal financial system—or with thin files—can be excluded if the models are not designed with diversity in mind. For millisecond credit to be equitable, it must be backed by broad data coverage, alternative data integrations, and fairness auditing to ensure that speed does not harden existing inequalities.

Nevertheless, the direction is clear. Businesses and individuals now operate in environments that move at digital speed. Their financial needs arise in real time and demand responses in kind. Whether managing cash flow during a late client payment, seizing an inventory discount that won't last, or responding to a crisis that demands immediate liquidity, borrowers need credit systems that operate at the pace of their lives. Millisecond architecture delivers on this need—not as a novelty, but as a foundational shift in how financial systems serve people.

The old underwriting model was built for deliberation, paper trails, and scheduled reviews. The new model is built for immediacy, data orchestration, and automated intelligence. Credit is no longer something applied for and awaited—it is something that is offered, structured, and delivered in the time it takes to blink. In this world, lending becomes a real-time service, integrated into the flow of commerce, available precisely when it is needed, and calibrated to the moment. That is the power of millisecond decision architecture. It is not just faster credit—it is a different kind of credit entirely, one shaped by the logic of now.

6.2 Pre-Approved Credit Ecosystems

The nature of credit is evolving from a system of application and approval to one of readiness and proactive availability. Traditional credit systems operate on demand; they wait for a request, then evaluate. But modern consumers and businesses are beginning to expect something different: frictionless access to credit that is already calculated, verified, and ready to activate at the point of need. This expectation has given rise to what can be described as pre-approved credit ecosystems—financial environments where users are continuously assessed, and credit is pre-positioned in anticipation of their needs rather than in response to them.

A pre-approved credit ecosystem is built on the foundation of continuous underwriting. Rather than evaluating a borrower once per application, these systems perform ongoing assessments using real-time data feeds, behavioral analytics, and dynamic risk modeling. Users are not prompted to submit a formal application each time they require financing. Instead, their financial behavior, cash flow trends, account activity, and even platform usage patterns are monitored with consent, and credit is automatically pre-calculated in the background. When the moment arises—whether it's a business replenishing inventory, an entrepreneur needing working capital, or a freelancer covering a temporary cash shortfall—the system is ready. Credit is not merely offered; it is embedded and waiting.

This always-on approach fundamentally changes the psychological relationship between the borrower and the lender. Instead of facing the barrier of uncertainty—Will I be approved? What documents are required? How long will it take?—the user is presented with clarity and immediacy: You are already approved. This shift removes friction, builds trust, and increases credit utilization without compromising risk management.

The emergence of these ecosystems is particularly evident in the rise of platform-based finance. Ecommerce marketplaces, payment processors, and accounting platforms are increasingly becoming credit providers—not by building banks, but by integrating lending directly into their ecosystems. Because these platforms already have granular visibility into user behavior, they can offer pre-approved credit with greater accuracy than traditional banks ever could. An ecommerce platform, for instance, can analyze a merchant's sales volume, refund rates, customer retention, and seasonality trends. Based on this data, it can pre-qualify the merchant for a loan, adjusting the offer dynamically as business conditions change. There's no need to ask for financial statements or wait for a credit score—everything needed for the decision is already in the platform's data stream.

This same model is taking shape in accounting software, payroll systems, logistics tools, and even industry-specific SaaS platforms. A construction software company might offer financing for material purchases based on project pipeline visibility. A booking platform might extend advances to hospitality businesses based on future reservation trends. In each case, the logic is the same: the platform knows the business, sees its cash flows, and can accurately assess its credit needs ahead of time.

The power of pre-approved credit ecosystems also lies in their ability to personalize. Because the systems are continuously analyzing data, they can tailor credit terms to fit the borrower's specific context. Repayment schedules can align with cash flow patterns. Interest rates can reflect real-time risk levels. Limits can scale up or down as business conditions evolve. This personalization is not just a nice-to-have—it is a critical advantage in risk mitigation. A business that receives funding on terms misaligned with its operational rhythm is more likely to struggle with repayment. Conversely, credit that adapts to the borrower's cycle is more likely to be repaid successfully.

Another dimension of these ecosystems is optionality. Users can be offered different types of credit at different stages of their lifecycle. A startup might begin with invoice factoring, move to working capital loans, and eventually qualify for growth-stage lines of credit. The platform's system, already familiar with the user's behavior, facilitates these transitions seamlessly. There is no need for reapplication or re-onboarding. Credit becomes an organic extension of business growth, not a bureaucratic hurdle to overcome.

Pre-approved credit ecosystems also facilitate responsible lending. Because they operate on continuous data, they can detect early signs of financial stress—declining revenue, rising expenses, payment delays—and respond proactively. Offers can be reduced, paused, or converted into structured repayment plans. This real-time adaptability allows lenders to manage portfolio risk more effectively while offering support to borrowers before defaults occur. The result is a more humane, responsive credit system—one that protects both parties without resorting to punitive measures.

Regulatory frameworks are beginning to catch up with this shift. Consent mechanisms, data governance rules, and fair lending practices are being redefined for continuous assessment environments. Borrowers must be informed of how their data is used, how decisions are made, and how to contest or opt out. Transparency and explainability become critical design features. Borrowers should be able to see why they've been approved, how their limit is calculated, and what behaviors might impact their future access.

Importantly, pre-approved ecosystems are not confined to large platforms. Smaller lenders, cooperatives, and credit unions can also adopt this model by partnering with fintech providers that offer real-time risk engines, data aggregation tools, and embedded credit modules. This democratizes access to innovation, allowing even community-focused institutions to offer cutting-edge services without needing to build entire infrastructures from scratch.

The future of credit is anticipatory. As data becomes richer and systems become smarter, lending will move further away from reactive models and toward preemptive engagement. Borrowers will not wait to be evaluated—they will live in financial environments where they are already known, understood, and supported. Credit will not begin with an application. It will begin with trust, maintained through continuous observation, and expressed through immediate, adaptive offers. This is the promise of pre-approved ecosystems: a world where capital flows at the speed of opportunity, tailored to the needs of the moment, and delivered without the friction of the past.

6.3 Mobile-First Credit Applications

The mobile phone has become the central hub of modern life. It is not just a tool for communication—it is a wallet, a bank, a business dashboard, and a social storefront. In the developing world, it is often the only access point to the digital economy. In developed markets, it is the preferred one. As a result, any credit system that does not prioritize mobile access is not only outdated—it is irrelevant to a growing majority of the population. The rise of mobile-first credit applications reflects a deeper shift: a redefinition of where, how, and for whom credit is made available.

Mobile-first design goes beyond simply shrinking a desktop experience to fit a smaller screen. It requires rethinking the entire user journey—how credit is discovered, understood, applied for, and managed—through the lens of the mobile device. This means optimizing for tap-based navigation, limited bandwidth, varied screen sizes, and diverse levels of digital literacy. But it also means leveraging the unique capabilities of mobile devices—such as GPS, biometric authentication, camera functionality, and instant messaging—to create a richer, more intuitive credit experience.

For many users, especially those in rural or underserved areas, the mobile phone is the only point of contact with financial services. Traditional branches may be distant, unreliable, or intimidating. Desktops may be unavailable. But with a phone in hand, a user can apply for a loan, submit identity documents, verify income, receive approval, and access funds—all without leaving their home or shop. This has made mobile-first credit applications a cornerstone of financial inclusion efforts across Africa, Southeast Asia, Latin America, and beyond.

These applications are often lightweight, fast-loading, and designed to work in low-connectivity environments. They prioritize simplicity and clarity. Instead of asking for detailed forms, they request consent to access phone metadata, mobile money history, or platform usage behavior. They use progressive disclosure—revealing more fields only when needed—to reduce user fatigue. And they speak the local language, culturally and literally, using familiar terms, formats, and tone. Some use voice prompts, chatbots, or even video tutorials to guide users through the process.

But mobile-first credit is not just for the underbanked. In advanced economies, consumers increasingly expect credit experiences that match the speed and convenience of other mobile services. A shopper comparing prices in a store might scan a QR code and receive an instant Buy Now Pay Later offer on their phone. A freelancer checking their earnings on a gig platform might tap a button and receive an advance based on verified income. A restaurant owner might use a mobile POS device that automatically offers working capital based on weekly sales. These moments depend on mobile-native credit experiences that are responsive, contextual, and seamlessly integrated into the flow of daily life.

Security and trust are paramount in mobile-first lending. The device must become a secure channel for identity verification, consent management, and fraud detection. Biometric authentication—fingerprint, face ID, or voice recognition—provides strong user validation. Device fingerprinting can help detect stolen or compromised phones. Geolocation can flag anomalies or confirm local business operations. Camera access allows users to submit real-time photos of inventory, premises, or documentation for verification. These tools, used ethically and transparently, build confidence while reducing reliance on paperwork.

Repayment also benefits from mobile integration. Notifications remind users of upcoming due dates. In-app payments allow for one-click repayment via linked accounts. Digital wallets can auto-debit scheduled installments. Users can track loan balances, see payment history, and access support—often through embedded chat or voice channels. The mobile interface becomes not just a place to apply for credit, but a dashboard for financial management, education, and engagement.

Mobile-first credit also supports behavioral lending models. Because the device captures so much data—app usage, transaction history, mobility patterns—credit scoring can adapt to new paradigms. A user's phone-based behaviors, when ethically processed with consent, can signal reliability. Consistent phone top-ups, regular messaging patterns, or location stability may correlate with responsible financial behavior. These signals, though unconventional, offer a bridge for those without traditional credit histories to gain access.

However, designing truly inclusive mobile-first applications requires care. Not all users are equally comfortable with technology. Some may fear digital scams or misunderstand the terms of an offer. Others may share devices with family members, complicating authentication. Designers must account for these realities by building in consent verification, multi-user safety features, and educational components that promote financial literacy. A successful mobile-first experience is not just accessible—it is understandable and empowering.

The future of mobile-first credit is likely to converge with other innovations. Voice assistants may offer spoken credit updates in local dialects. Augmented reality may help visualize payment plans or show inventory impacts. Offline functionality may allow remote users to apply for loans and sync data later. Cross-app integration may enable users to manage loans across marketplaces, utility platforms, or social apps.

In all these cases, the key is responsiveness—not just in terms of speed, but in terms of meeting people where they are, with tools that fit into their lives. The mobile device, ubiquitous and personal, becomes the ideal medium for this kind of interaction. It is always on, always near, and increasingly central to economic participation.

As we move into this mobile-centric future, the question is no longer whether mobile-first credit is viable—it is how fast lenders can adapt. The generation entering the workforce today will expect credit to be available on their devices, contextualized by their behavior, and delivered without delay. Businesses too, especially those operating in fast-moving or low-margin sectors, will demand financing solutions that are as nimble as their operations.

The mobile-first revolution is already underway. It is changing how people borrow, how lenders assess risk, and how capital moves through economies. It is expanding access, reducing barriers, and redefining what it means to participate in the financial system. And for those willing to innovate, it represents not just a channel, but an entirely new way of thinking about credit: not as an institution, but as an experience—personal, portable, and always within reach.

Chapter 7: Peer-to-Peer and Marketplace Lending Evolution

7.1 Institutional Capital Meets Retail Investors

Peer-to-peer (P2P) lending began with a radical premise: eliminate the bank. Let everyday individuals lend directly to others, matching surplus capital with unmet credit demand, facilitated not by an institution, but by a digital platform. It was hailed as democratization, as disintermediation, as the future of finance in its most decentralized form. In its early days, the model was personal and simple. A teacher in Ohio could lend $1,000 to a carpenter in Georgia. A retiree in the UK could fund a wedding florist in Edinburgh. The appeal lay in the human scale of it, the directness, the idea that finance could be rebuilt as a social contract, digitized but intimate. Borrowers benefited from streamlined processes and often better rates, while lenders found opportunities to earn yield outside the limitations of savings accounts or volatile equity markets.

Yet as the model matured, it encountered realities that reshaped its trajectory. Loan defaults, risk modeling challenges, regulatory scrutiny, and inconsistent underwriting practices forced platforms to refine, professionalize, and scale. And with that maturation came a profound shift: the arrival of institutional capital. What began as an experiment in grassroots finance began to attract hedge funds, pension managers, insurance companies, and family offices. These actors brought with them large pools of capital, sophisticated analytical tools, and a hunger for yield in a world of suppressed interest rates. The P2P model—once niche and amateur—was now drawing the attention of serious players.

This convergence marked the beginning of a new chapter in marketplace lending, one defined by the synthesis of institutional rigor and retail accessibility.

The entry of institutional investors into peer-based lending platforms changed everything. Retail lenders, accustomed to selecting individual loans or funding borrowers manually, began to find themselves operating alongside algorithmic funds that deployed capital at scale, often with access to privileged data or direct platform integrations. Platforms, in turn, began tailoring products to these deep-pocketed participants. Whole loan sales, forward flow agreements, and customized portfolio tranches became standard offerings. Instead of thousands of small investors funding micro-loans, large institutions began buying up loan originations in bulk—sometimes the majority of them.

This shift introduced a delicate tension. On one hand, institutional capital provided liquidity, credibility, and a stabilizing force. It allowed platforms to expand faster, lend more aggressively, and invest in better technology and compliance systems. On the other hand, it challenged the original ethos of the model. The more professionalized and scaled the system became, the less "peer-to-peer" it felt. Retail investors began to question their role. Were they still valued participants in a democratized finance movement, or merely window dressing for an increasingly institutional machine?

Some platforms responded by bifurcating their offerings. Retail investors received access to curated loan pools or simplified investment products, while institutional clients were offered custom APIs, private deals, and tailored risk exposures. Others went further, pivoting entirely to institutional capital and exiting the retail space. LendingClub, once the poster child of the P2P movement, eventually became a digital bank. Prosper refocused on institutional partnerships. Across the industry, what began as a decentralized experiment gradually centralized around large pools of money and the platforms that served them.

Yet this evolution did not erase the role of retail investors. In fact, their presence remains vital for reasons both strategic and philosophical. Retail capital offers a kind of resilience. It is more stable in certain downturns, more emotionally committed, and more patient than hot institutional money. Platforms that balance both sources of capital often find themselves better insulated against shocks. Moreover, retail investors help maintain the original narrative—that lending can be a human endeavor, not just a financial algorithm. Many still choose loans based on borrower stories, purposes, or shared geographies. The emotional engagement of the retail investor is a counterweight to the cold logic of institutional spreadsheets.

The convergence of institutional and retail capital has also led to hybrid financial products that blend characteristics of both. Fractionalized loans, automated investment plans, thematic credit portfolios, and marketplace lending funds allow smaller investors to benefit from institutional-grade risk modeling without having to analyze every individual borrower. Conversely, institutions have begun using machine learning and behavioral analytics to identify retail lending patterns that outperform—insights born from intuition, not just data.

Technology has enabled this synthesis. Advanced portfolio engines, real-time data feeds, and modular investment dashboards allow platforms to serve both retail and institutional audiences from the same core infrastructure. APIs provide high-frequency access for institutions, while mobile apps offer guided simplicity for individual users. Behind the scenes, a single loan may be funded by a mix of capital sources—each with its own yield expectations, risk appetite, and liquidity profile.

Regulators have also adapted, albeit cautiously. As marketplace lending gained prominence, financial authorities began to impose stricter disclosure requirements, capital adequacy standards, and borrower protections. In some jurisdictions, platforms were required to obtain banking licenses or form partnerships with chartered institutions. This increased scrutiny had a dual effect: it reduced some of the early inefficiencies and risks of P2P lending, but it also made the model more expensive and complex to operate. For institutional investors, these changes brought comfort and legitimacy. For retail participants, they sometimes created barriers—higher minimums, fewer choices, and more opaque decision-making.

Nevertheless, innovation continues. Blockchain and tokenization have introduced new possibilities. Some platforms are now exploring the idea of tokenized loan pools, where retail and institutional investors alike can purchase fractional interests in credit products represented as digital assets. These structures allow for secondary trading, improved liquidity, and real-time settlement—features that benefit all participants, regardless of scale. Smart contracts automate repayments, dividend distributions, and compliance, reducing administrative costs and increasing transparency. This technological layer may yet restore some of the decentralization originally envisioned in early P2P platforms.

Another area of innovation lies in geographic expansion. As traditional credit markets in developed countries saturate, institutional and retail capital alike are being directed toward emerging markets, where credit access remains limited but mobile adoption is high. Platforms that connect global lenders with local borrowers, using mobile data, social credit scoring, and alternative payment infrastructure, are redefining what cross-border lending can look like. In these environments, the partnership between institutional scale and retail compassion becomes even more critical. Institutions bring capital, risk systems, and operational rigor. Retail investors bring attention, storytelling, and mission alignment.

Perhaps most importantly, the blending of institutional and retail capital in marketplace lending is forcing a reevaluation of the role platforms play. Are they simply conduits, matching supply with demand? Or are they curators, gatekeepers, co-lenders, or something else entirely? As platforms assume greater responsibility for loan performance, compliance, and user experience, they move from being neutral marketplaces to active financial institutions in their own right. This evolution mirrors that of stock exchanges, which began as passive venues but now provide liquidity, analytics, and risk management tools.

In the future, we may see more collaborative credit ecosystems, where institutional and retail investors co-fund loans transparently, with shared dashboards, co-investment strategies, and dynamic risk-sharing agreements. Platforms may offer modular investment blocks, allowing individuals to "stack" their exposure—combining a base of institutional-grade auto-lending, a layer of thematic retail portfolios, and a topping of personalized handpicked loans. This model aligns the interests of all participants, enhances diversification, and turns lending into a more participatory, creative act.

Ultimately, the meeting of institutional capital and retail investors within the marketplace lending ecosystem reflects the broader narrative of financial transformation. It is a story of democratization meeting professionalization, of ideals evolving into infrastructure, and of systems designed for people becoming systems managed by algorithms—yet still shaped by human intention. Peer-to-peer lending was never just about removing the bank. It was about reimagining trust. In this new chapter, that trust is mediated not only by code and compliance but by a shared willingness—from both retail and institutional participants—to create a lending environment that is faster, smarter, fairer, and more responsive to the needs of a connected world.

7.2 Specialized Vertical Marketplaces

The evolution of peer-to-peer and marketplace lending has not followed a linear path—it has fractured, specialized, and reorganized itself around the particularities of industries, communities, and financial use cases. As the broader marketplace model matured, a new wave of platforms emerged with a different focus: depth over breadth. Rather than trying to be everything to everyone, these platforms are building lending ecosystems tailored to specific sectors—what are now referred to as *specialized vertical marketplaces*. In these purpose-built environments, every component of the lending experience—risk assessment, underwriting logic, funding structures, and borrower-lender interaction—is optimized for the dynamics of one specific domain.

The rationale behind vertical specialization is rooted in nuance. Generalized lending platforms, by design, must normalize diverse types of credit demand into standardized products. A restaurant seeking equipment financing, a rideshare driver requesting working capital, and a freelance developer funding a new laptop might all be offered similar products based on common denominators such as credit score or repayment history. But these common metrics often flatten the rich context that defines each use case. Specialized vertical marketplaces, on the other hand, are designed to *lean into* that complexity. They recognize that underwriting a dental clinic is different from underwriting a short-term rental operator. That a seasonal farm has different cash flow patterns than a SaaS startup. And that a trucking company's creditworthiness might be more accurately judged by fleet utilization data than by a bank statement.

In a vertical marketplace, both data and relationships become highly contextualized. Consider a platform built specifically for construction businesses. It would not merely replicate generic loan offerings—it would integrate with project management software like Procore, sync with invoice cycles from subcontractors, assess bidding history, and understand permitting timelines. A lender operating in this context could evaluate a borrower not just as a credit applicant, but as a contractor with real, measurable, operational performance. This insight leads to smarter lending decisions and more appropriately structured terms—perhaps with repayment schedules aligned to milestone-based construction draws, or collateral structured against pending receivables from city contracts.

Likewise, in the world of ecommerce, specialized marketplaces have begun underwriting based on real-time sales, product return rates, customer feedback scores, and advertising efficiency metrics. These platforms might integrate with Shopify or Amazon Seller Central, pulling granular data that no traditional underwriter would ever see. A seller launching a new product line could be offered a short-term inventory financing package, underwritten dynamically based on historical conversion rates and seasonality trends. This type of credit is not only more relevant—it's more likely to be used effectively, and therefore, more likely to be repaid.

Another growing vertical is the creator economy. Freelancers, digital content producers, and independent service providers often lack formal credit profiles but have high-income potential. Vertical platforms that specialize in this market use unique data sources—Patreon donations, Substack subscriptions, Instagram engagement rates, and platform payouts from YouTube or TikTok. Some even assess consistency in content production as a proxy for income reliability. These insights would be invisible to conventional financial systems, yet they are critical in evaluating a creator's financial health.

Beyond risk modeling, vertical specialization offers cultural and operational advantages. Borrowers tend to trust platforms that "speak their language," that understand their challenges, seasonality, and workflows. When a platform builds interfaces, onboarding flows, and customer support with the vocabulary and rhythms of a specific industry, it creates an experience that feels designed rather than adapted. A farmer applying for a loan through a platform that references crop cycles, weather risk, and cooperative partnerships will feel more understood than if they were dealing with a generic credit portal asking for generic data. That trust translates into stronger engagement, higher application conversion, and more sustainable repayment behavior.

On the investor side, vertical platforms can attract capital that is aligned with specific sectors or impact themes. For example, a green energy lending platform can appeal to climate-conscious investors seeking to fund solar installations, EV infrastructure, or energy efficiency upgrades. A platform focused on women-owned businesses can attract funds with gender-lens investing mandates. Because the data within a vertical is more consistent and performance patterns more predictable, risk models can be calibrated more precisely, and investors can deploy capital with greater confidence.

Vertical marketplaces also allow for tighter integration with ecosystem partners. A platform serving small restaurants might partner with point-of-sale providers, food delivery networks, or supplier cooperatives. These integrations allow for better data, richer underwriting, and embedded repayment mechanisms— such as loan repayments deducted automatically from daily sales or food delivery revenues. This ecosystem-centric model blurs the line between lender, platform, and operator, creating a tightly woven financial fabric that supports businesses not just with money, but with tools, insights, and community.

The scalability of vertical marketplaces does not lie in expanding horizontally into other sectors, but in deepening their presence within a domain. That might mean expanding geographically, developing new product tiers (such as lease financing, revenue-based lending, or invoice factoring), or layering on services like business coaching, insurance, or procurement support. These platforms become more than lenders—they become sector-specific operating systems for financial health and growth.

As the future of lending continues to fragment into personalized experiences, the vertical marketplace model is likely to proliferate. What was once a monolithic credit industry is evolving into a constellation of niche platforms, each optimized for a type of borrower, a type of data, and a type of capital. This fragmentation is not chaotic—it's adaptive. It reflects the reality that lending, at its best, is a relationship between understanding and trust. And trust, in the modern world, is often built not by being broad, but by being deeply specific.

7.3 Hybrid Marketplace Models

As the credit landscape continues to transform, a new breed of platform is emerging—one that seeks to combine the best of multiple models into a single, adaptive ecosystem. These are the *hybrid marketplace models*, a fusion of traditional and digital finance, of peer and institutional capital, of vertical specialization and horizontal scalability. In these platforms, no single ideology dominates. Instead, design is guided by flexibility: the ability to adapt to different borrower types, funding sources, regulatory environments, and economic cycles. This agility is not accidental—it is a deliberate architectural choice born from the recognition that no single lending model is sufficient for the complexity of today's credit markets.

At the core of hybrid models is modular infrastructure. These platforms are built like financial toolkits, capable of offering different lending experiences based on who is participating and what is being financed. A small business owner might receive a loan funded by a pool of retail investors, structured via smart contracts, and underwritten using traditional cash flow data. A larger borrower might access institutional credit packaged through forward flow agreements, with repayment terms tailored by machine learning models. The same platform can serve both ends of the spectrum, not by flattening differences, but by recognizing and encoding them into its operating system.

Hybrid marketplaces often maintain both retail-facing and institution-facing interfaces. For retail participants, they might offer pre-packaged investment products, automated loan diversification tools, or thematic bundles focused on ESG goals, regional development, or sector-specific lending. For institutions, the same loans might be available via API, with custom analytics, real-time reporting, and negotiated structures. This dual approach allows platforms to tap into the emotional engagement and marketing reach of retail communities while leveraging the scale, discipline, and capital stability of professional investors.

One powerful feature of hybrid models is the ability to channel capital dynamically. For instance, if institutional liquidity contracts during a macroeconomic downturn, the platform can lean more heavily on its retail base, offering yield opportunities aligned with market demand. Conversely, if retail appetite wanes due to market volatility, institutions can provide a steady floor of capital. The platform thus becomes a dynamic allocator, continuously optimizing funding flows, risk exposures, and pricing based on evolving conditions.

From a borrower perspective, hybrid models increase optionality and resilience. A borrower might begin with a peer-funded microloan, graduate to an AI-powered working capital facility, and eventually access mezzanine financing structured with institutional co-lenders. Each product, each stage, is housed within the same ecosystem. Borrowers don't need to reapply, re-verify, or migrate data—they evolve within a platform that grows with them. This continuity improves loyalty, reduces churn, and allows the platform to collect deeper longitudinal data, which in turn improves risk models and cross-sell capabilities.

Technologically, hybrid marketplaces tend to operate on multi-layered architectures that support both permissioned and permissionless transactions. Blockchain may be used for settlement and transparency, while proprietary scoring engines handle risk analysis. Smart contracts may automate repayments, but traditional legal frameworks remain in place for enforcement. The point is not to choose between Web2 and Web3 paradigms— but to borrow strategically from both, depending on use case, jurisdiction, and participant preference.

Hybrid models are also at the forefront of regulatory adaptation. Because they serve diverse participants—some of whom are highly regulated and others who are not—they must maintain flexible compliance frameworks. That might mean embedding KYC and AML at multiple touchpoints, dynamically adjusting disclosures based on investor sophistication, or complying with multiple national regulations simultaneously. Some platforms now offer "compliance layers," allowing them to adapt operations to local requirements while maintaining a single global engine. This modular compliance is not just a defensive strategy—it becomes a competitive advantage as platforms expand internationally.

Culturally, hybrid platforms are shaped by pragmatism. They are less idealistic than early P2P platforms, less monolithic than traditional banks, and less dogmatic than pure DeFi projects. Instead, they are builders—engineering systems that work under real-world constraints. They recognize that borrowers care less about the ideology behind the capital and more about the reliability, speed, and fairness of access. They understand that investors want yield, but also transparency, liquidity, and risk-adjusted returns. And they know that regulators want innovation—but within frameworks that protect users and preserve stability.

One of the most promising aspects of hybrid models is their capacity for cross-sector collaboration. A hybrid platform might partner with a logistics company to finance last-mile delivery fleets while simultaneously working with a municipal agency to deploy impact capital for local businesses. These platforms can absorb multiple mandates—commercial, social, environmental—without sacrificing coherence. They are not just financial actors; they are network orchestrators, connecting capital with opportunity in ways that are both scalable and sensitive to context.

As credit becomes increasingly embedded into digital life—offered at checkout, inside apps, via APIs, through voice assistants—the importance of flexible, adaptive infrastructure cannot be overstated. Hybrid marketplaces are not trying to pick a winning model. They are trying to build systems that work in the messy, overlapping, multi-speed world of 21st-century finance. Their success lies not in purity, but in orchestration—the ability to pull from peer lending, institutional finance, vertical specialization, embedded credit, and decentralized technology to create something more durable, more accessible, and more intelligent than any of its predecessors.

In the years ahead, hybrid platforms may become the new default. Not because they are perfect, but because they are resilient. They learn from every model that came before—taking the peer-to-peer movement's spirit, the marketplace's scalability, the vertical specialist's precision, and the institution's scale—and fusing them into ecosystems that can evolve as fast as the world around them. In a time of accelerating change, that kind of adaptability may be the only true competitive edge.

Chapter 8: Regulatory Technology (RegTech) in Lending

8.1 Automated Compliance Monitoring

The digital transformation of lending has ushered in a new era of operational complexity. As fintech platforms, neobanks, peer-to-peer marketplaces, and embedded finance ecosystems accelerate the speed and scale of credit delivery, they also multiply the number of regulatory obligations they must meet. Across jurisdictions and sectors, compliance is no longer a checklist at the end of a process—it is a dynamic, continuous, and integral part of the lending lifecycle. In this context, *automated compliance monitoring* has emerged as one of the most crucial applications of Regulatory Technology (RegTech). It is not just about obeying the law; it is about building systems that understand, interpret, and act on legal and regulatory obligations in real time, without sacrificing speed, user experience, or innovation.

Traditionally, compliance has been a reactive and labor-intensive function. Risk and legal teams would periodically audit transactions, review documents, and cross-reference regulations manually. Even in more digitized institutions, much of the compliance function has relied on static rules-based systems prone to both over-flagging (false positives) and under-flagging (missed violations). This model is not only inefficient—it is also fundamentally misaligned with the pace and complexity of modern digital lending, where thousands of transactions may be processed in real time, across multiple regions, currencies, and product types. In such a dynamic environment, the old compliance model creates bottlenecks, increases risk, and introduces friction into user experience.

Automated compliance monitoring, powered by RegTech innovations, represents a paradigm shift. It reimagines compliance not as a policing function, but as an embedded intelligence system—capable of interpreting regulatory language, monitoring behavior, and triggering alerts or actions automatically based on dynamic rule sets. These systems ingest regulatory updates as they happen, parse them using natural language processing, and translate them into machine-executable logic. Once integrated into lending platforms, they can monitor a vast range of variables—from borrower behavior and transaction patterns to contractual obligations and geographic constraints—with a level of precision and speed that human teams simply cannot match.

One of the core strengths of automated compliance systems lies in their ability to manage *regulatory heterogeneity*. A digital lending platform operating across different states or countries must comply with a patchwork of overlapping rules, each with its own licensing requirements, disclosure mandates, interest rate caps, anti-money laundering (AML) standards, and privacy laws. Manual tracking of these obligations is not only time-consuming—it is dangerously error-prone. Automated systems, on the other hand, can be configured to flag when a loan offer in a certain ZIP code triggers a state-specific usury law, or when a transaction involving a foreign currency requires enhanced due diligence under cross-border finance rules. This contextual monitoring ensures compliance without requiring human agents to memorize thousands of regulatory clauses or build ad hoc processes every time a rule changes.

More importantly, these systems are not static. They evolve. Machine learning models trained on historical compliance cases can identify patterns of non-compliance or near misses, helping platforms preemptively adjust their processes. For example, if a particular type of borrower tends to fall into a category that triggers enhanced scrutiny under consumer protection laws, the system can automatically insert additional disclosures, modify product terms, or flag the transaction for review—all in real time, and without disrupting the borrower's experience. This proactive model reduces the risk of regulatory violations while improving transparency and fairness in lending.

The automation of compliance also opens the door to *continuous auditing*. Traditional audits are episodic, backward-looking exercises that rely on sampling and interpretation. Automated systems, however, can maintain a real-time audit trail for every transaction, decision, and system interaction. Every compliance check, every rule evaluation, every exception handling step is logged, time-stamped, and stored in immutable ledgers— sometimes even on blockchain infrastructures, depending on the architecture. This level of traceability not only simplifies audit preparation, but also strengthens the platform's ability to demonstrate regulatory integrity during investigations or due diligence processes. In a world of increasing regulatory scrutiny and data sovereignty debates, such real-time auditability is no longer a luxury—it is a requirement.

The application of artificial intelligence within automated compliance systems also transforms the way institutions understand and manage risk. By analyzing massive datasets in real time, these systems can detect anomalies that might indicate fraud, misreporting, or regulatory breaches. For example, a sudden change in a borrower's repayment behavior, inconsistent document metadata, or abnormal login patterns could signal deeper compliance issues. These anomalies can trigger automated workflows—such as freezing the transaction, notifying a compliance officer, or escalating to regulators if necessary. These automated interventions not only reduce operational risk but also demonstrate a lender's commitment to proactive governance.

Of course, the implementation of automated compliance systems is not without its challenges. One of the biggest hurdles is *regulatory interpretation.* Legal texts are often complex, ambiguous, and context-dependent. Translating these into machine-readable logic requires not only advanced natural language processing (NLP) capabilities but also collaboration between legal experts, compliance officers, and engineers. The system must understand when a rule is absolute versus when it allows for discretion. It must differentiate between legally binding obligations and regulatory guidance. And it must be able to update its rule sets when new laws are passed, cases are adjudicated, or agency priorities shift. This process, while technically demanding, is at the heart of RegTech's value proposition: turning legal complexity into programmable intelligence.

Another challenge lies in ensuring *explainability.* As regulators increasingly demand transparency in automated decision-making—especially in areas like credit scoring and fraud detection—compliance systems must not only make decisions but also justify them. If a loan is denied based on an AML risk flag, the platform must be able to articulate the logic behind the flag, the data used, and the regulatory rationale. This requirement for *explainable automation* is one reason many platforms are integrating *hybrid models*—combining rule-based engines with supervised machine learning to balance precision with traceability. In highly sensitive areas, some platforms even use *human-in-the-loop* systems, where automation does the heavy lifting but human experts make final calls on edge cases.

Furthermore, data governance becomes critically important in an automated compliance environment. These systems require access to vast datasets—customer profiles, behavioral histories, transaction records, geolocation data, third-party risk databases—all of which are subject to privacy regulations such as GDPR, CCPA, and others. Automated compliance systems must therefore be built with privacy-by-design principles: granular consent mechanisms, data minimization strategies, encryption protocols, and mechanisms to ensure that data used for compliance is not repurposed without authorization. In fact, many platforms now use RegTech not only to enforce external laws, but also to enforce their *internal data ethics policies*, which increasingly serve as a competitive differentiator in privacy-conscious markets.

The economic impact of automated compliance is also worth noting. By reducing the cost and latency of compliance, RegTech enables lenders to scale faster, serve more diverse customer segments, and experiment with new product models without running afoul of regulators. For startups and non-bank lenders, this means being able to compete with incumbents without needing to build massive legal departments. For traditional banks, it means reducing overhead, streamlining legacy processes, and accelerating digital transformation. In many cases, the savings from automated compliance can be reinvested into customer experience, product innovation, or expanded underwriting capabilities—creating a virtuous cycle of efficiency and growth.

Perhaps the most profound implication of automated compliance monitoring is cultural. In legacy institutions, compliance has often been siloed—a reactive department that says "no" after the fact. With automation, compliance becomes *embedded*—not an obstacle, but an enabler. It is integrated into code, into user flows, into product design. Engineers no longer need to "check with legal" before shipping a feature—they can consult the compliance layer of the codebase. Product managers no longer need to guess whether a new lending structure is compliant—they can test it in simulation against the rule engine. This shift transforms compliance from a friction point into a design constraint—one that, when embraced early, leads to cleaner, safer, and more trustworthy systems.

Looking ahead, automated compliance will become increasingly intelligent, predictive, and autonomous. Systems will not just monitor for breaches—they will *forecast* regulatory risks, simulate potential violations, and recommend proactive mitigations. They will serve not just as watchdogs, but as advisors—alerting platforms to shifts in enforcement priorities, proposing changes to underwriting rules, or identifying jurisdictions where new licenses might be needed. This transformation will be powered by ongoing advances in AI, but also by deeper collaboration between regulators and technologists. Already, some jurisdictions are experimenting with *regulatory sandboxes* that allow platforms to test automated compliance systems under supervised conditions. Others are exploring the idea of *machine-readable regulation*, where laws are published in formats designed to be ingested directly by RegTech engines.

In the long arc of financial innovation, automated compliance monitoring may come to be seen not as a side note, but as a foundational shift. It is not merely a tool for avoiding penalties— it is a mechanism for earning trust, scaling responsibly, and navigating complexity with confidence. As lending becomes faster, more personalized, and more embedded in digital life, compliance must follow suit. It must become faster, more intelligent, and more integrated. Automated compliance monitoring is the path to that future—a future in which innovation and regulation are not at odds, but in dialogue, mediated by systems that are always watching, always learning, and always working to keep the promise of fair, lawful, and ethical finance alive.

8.2 Fair Lending Algorithm Auditing

As algorithmic decision-making systems become central to the modern credit industry, questions of fairness, accountability, and transparency have moved from philosophical debates to urgent regulatory concerns. Nowhere is this more evident than in the domain of fair lending—a space traditionally governed by laws intended to prevent discrimination based on race, gender, age, geography, or socioeconomic status. In the analog era, compliance with these principles was relatively straightforward, enforced through standardized forms, paper trails, and visible human judgments. But with the rise of artificial intelligence and machine learning in underwriting, the challenge has grown exponentially more complex. Algorithms do not simply mimic human behavior—they scale it, amplify it, and evolve it over time. Without rigorous oversight, they can also encode and propagate hidden biases with chilling precision. This is the crucible in which the practice of fair lending algorithm auditing is being forged: as a new class of regulatory technology, legal mandate, and ethical imperative.

At its core, algorithm auditing in lending means evaluating the decision-making logic of AI-driven systems to ensure they do not produce disparate outcomes across protected classes. But auditing an algorithm is not like auditing a bank ledger. These systems are often opaque, especially when built using deep learning or other high-dimensional modeling techniques. Their inner workings cannot be easily expressed as a set of if-then rules or clearly defined parameters. The same model might produce acceptable outcomes in one context but manifest unintentional bias when applied to different data populations. Worse, a model that uses "neutral" variables such as zip code, educational attainment, or browser type might still end up discriminating indirectly, due to correlations with race, income, or national origin. This phenomenon, known as proxy discrimination, is at the heart of the regulatory challenge.

To address this complexity, auditors of fair lending algorithms are now developing multi-disciplinary frameworks that combine statistical analysis, legal reasoning, and systems engineering. A typical audit may begin with a **dataset audit**—assessing whether the data used to train a lending algorithm is balanced across demographic groups. If certain communities are underrepresented in the training set, the model may fail to learn their behavior patterns accurately, leading to higher default assumptions or lower approval rates. This data imbalance can arise innocently—for example, a fintech startup focused on urban millennials may have few data points for older rural populations—but it results in systematic exclusion nonetheless. Algorithmic fairness begins, therefore, not with the code but with the corpus it learns from.

Next, auditors assess the **performance parity** of the model: does it produce similar approval rates, default predictions, and interest rate recommendations across different demographic segments, assuming similar financial profiles? If two applicants with identical incomes, credit histories, and employment status receive different outcomes solely because of demographic variables, that's a clear red flag. But even when demographic variables are not directly input into the model, disparities may still occur indirectly. Modern auditing tools therefore use techniques like counterfactual analysis, where hypothetical versions of each application are tested with altered demographics to detect outcome sensitivity. If changing an applicant's race or gender significantly shifts the predicted risk or loan terms, the algorithm is exhibiting unfair bias—even if that variable was never explicitly used.

Another layer of auditing involves **explainability**—a requirement not just for regulators, but for affected borrowers. If an applicant is denied credit by an AI system, they have the legal right to understand why. This is enshrined in laws like the Equal Credit Opportunity Act (ECOA) in the U.S. and similar frameworks in Europe. However, many AI models cannot provide human-readable explanations for their decisions. This has led to the development of explainable AI (XAI) frameworks tailored for credit models, which can generate rationale summaries, feature importance scores, or natural language justifications for loan decisions. These explanations are then tested during audits to ensure they are consistent, accurate, and not misleading.

Importantly, fair lending audits are not one-time events. Algorithms continue to learn and adapt over time—especially those using online or real-time learning. This means that even a model that was fair at launch can drift toward biased behavior as its inputs or environmental context shift. Continuous monitoring is therefore essential. Some platforms now implement **live fairness dashboards** that track algorithmic behavior across demographics in real time, flagging any deviation from expected parity. Others simulate new lending scenarios using synthetic populations to ensure ongoing equity across evolving applicant types.

Despite these advances, a cultural challenge remains. Many technologists and data scientists view regulatory constraints as a hindrance to innovation, while many legal experts see algorithms as inherently suspect. Auditing for fair lending success requires bridging this divide. Regulators must become more literate in AI, while developers must internalize fairness as a non-negotiable design constraint—not an afterthought or a compliance burden. Encouragingly, a new generation of fintech startups is embracing this mindset, building fairness-first systems from the ground up and engaging independent ethics boards or community review panels to oversee their algorithmic practices.

Regulators, too, are adapting. In the U.S., the Consumer Financial Protection Bureau (CFPB) has signaled its intent to enforce fair lending laws even when violations arise from AI systems that use proxies for protected characteristics. The European Union's proposed AI Act includes provisions for "high-risk" AI systems—including those used in lending—requiring transparency, human oversight, and bias mitigation. Similar frameworks are emerging in Canada, Australia, Singapore, and Latin America, creating a patchwork of global norms that reinforce the central message: fairness is not optional. If you build a model that denies someone credit, you must prove that decision was justifiable—not just statistically, but ethically.

In the future, algorithm auditing may evolve even further—from rule-based evaluation to real-time accountability ecosystems. Borrowers may be given tools to see how their data was interpreted, how their risk score was derived, and how alternative data might improve their standing. Platforms may offer *credit simulations*, where applicants can preview likely outcomes and receive guidance on how to improve them. Regulators may begin certifying not just models, but entire lending platforms based on their fairness track record, transparency, and responsiveness to community feedback. In this world, the audit is not an adversarial process—it is a feature of trustworthy finance.

8.3 Cross-Border Regulatory Harmonization

As the global economy becomes more digitally integrated, lending is no longer a local business. A fintech platform based in Berlin may serve borrowers in Nairobi, while investors in Singapore fund microloans in rural Brazil. This globalization of credit brings enormous opportunities: it allows capital to flow more efficiently, enables credit access in underbanked regions, and fosters innovation through competition and diversity. But it also introduces a formidable challenge—navigating the labyrinth of legal systems, licensing requirements, and compliance obligations that differ from country to country. In this context, cross-border regulatory harmonization has emerged as both a necessity and a strategic advantage. It is the process of aligning—or at least reconciling—regulatory frameworks across jurisdictions to enable safe, fair, and efficient cross-border lending.

Historically, financial regulation has been a fiercely local affair. Banking licenses, consumer protections, data residency rules, and tax structures are all shaped by national priorities and political histories. Even within closely integrated regions like the European Union, differences remain in how lending rules are interpreted and enforced. For example, while the EU has harmonized consumer disclosure standards through directives like CCD (Consumer Credit Directive), national regulators often impose additional layers of interpretation or licensing requirements. Outside of these blocks, the divergence is even starker. A fintech offering credit in India must comply with Reserve Bank of India guidelines, while the same product in the United States falls under federal rules from the CFPB and a thicket of state-level statutes. Navigating this complexity is daunting, especially for startups or platforms seeking to scale rapidly across borders.

To solve this, several approaches to harmonization are emerging. One is the use of **regulatory sandboxes**—jurisdiction-specific programs that allow platforms to test new financial products under relaxed regulatory oversight, with the intention of informing future policy. These sandboxes, now active in over 60 countries, create a space for experimentation while fostering dialogue between innovators and regulators. When multiple countries collaborate on sandbox initiatives—such as in ASEAN or the Gulf Cooperation Council—they also begin to align definitions, risk thresholds, and evaluation metrics, paving the way for eventual harmonization.

Another major driver of alignment is the rise of **global data standards**. Open banking frameworks, for example, often adopt shared API schemas and authentication protocols. If platforms in multiple countries follow the same technical standards for accessing and sharing financial data, then regulatory bodies can more easily coordinate oversight, ensure interoperability, and enforce consumer protections. Groups like the International Organization for Standardization (ISO), the Financial Stability Board (FSB), and regional fintech associations are actively developing taxonomies and guidelines to support this convergence. As data becomes the foundation of credit decisioning, having shared language and structure is a prerequisite for safe global operations.

Multilateral treaties and **model laws** also contribute to harmonization. Organizations like UNCITRAL and the World Bank have developed model legal frameworks for digital finance, which countries can adapt to local contexts. These models don't impose uniformity, but they create a common foundation— clarifying definitions of digital identity, outlining permissible lending practices, and establishing cross-border enforcement mechanisms. As more countries adopt these templates, the regulatory landscape begins to resemble a patchwork quilt with aligned seams rather than a chaotic tangle.

Yet harmonization is not about making every jurisdiction the same. Rather, it is about creating **mutual recognitions** and safe operational corridors. Just as drivers can use their licenses across borders under agreed conditions, lenders might one day operate across jurisdictions if they meet equivalent standards for data protection, capital reserves, and ethical AI use. Already, some regions are experimenting with "passporting" regimes, where licenses or compliance credentials in one country are accepted in another. If this model scales, it could dramatically reduce the cost and friction of global expansion.

The most successful platforms will not wait for full harmonization to occur. Instead, they are building **compliance orchestration engines** that adapt dynamically to each jurisdiction. These engines ingest local laws, generate contextual disclosures, enforce geo-fenced rule sets, and produce audit trails customized to regulatory expectations. At the same time, they monitor global shifts—such as new data laws in Brazil or AI ethics rules in Canada—updating internal policies in near real-time. These systems turn regulatory diversity into a competitive advantage: the more jurisdictions a platform can navigate confidently, the broader its market access, investor confidence, and borrower trust.

In the coming years, we may see the emergence of **regulatory nodes**—jurisdictions that act as cross-border compliance hubs. Just as Delaware became a global hub for corporate registration, or Luxembourg for fund domiciling, new digital finance jurisdictions may arise, offering robust oversight, high-quality infrastructure, and alignment with international norms. Platforms operating from these nodes could act as global conduits for capital, data, and innovation, subject to strong governance and international cooperation.

Ultimately, cross-border regulatory harmonization is about building trust at scale. It ensures that a borrower in one country is protected by the same principles as a borrower in another— even if the platforms, currencies, or legal systems differ. It reassures investors that their capital is being deployed in environments where risk is understood and managed responsibly. And it empowers regulators to collaborate across borders, recognizing that financial systems are now interconnected ecosystems, not national silos. In a world where capital knows no borders, regulation must learn to travel just as well.

Chapter 9: Cybersecurity and Risk Management in Digital Lending

9.1 Zero-Trust Security Architecture

As digital lending platforms continue to redefine the financial ecosystem—replacing manual credit decisions with real-time automation, embedding credit into mobile applications, and connecting borrowers and lenders across continents—they inevitably become high-value targets for cyber threats. These platforms do not merely store sensitive financial data; they operate as trust engines that mediate access to money, identity, and opportunity. Every transaction, every loan decision, every API call carries with it an implicit expectation of integrity, confidentiality, and continuity. To meet that expectation in an increasingly hostile digital environment, forward-thinking platforms are abandoning outdated perimeter-based security models in favor of a new paradigm: zero-trust security architecture.

The zero-trust model represents a fundamental rethinking of how digital systems are protected. Traditional cybersecurity approaches operate on the assumption that systems can be divided into "inside" and "outside"—with firewalls and authentication gates at the edges keeping out malicious actors. Once inside the network, users and services are often granted broad privileges, implicitly trusted to act in good faith. But in today's distributed, API-driven, cloud-native lending environments, that assumption is dangerously obsolete. Attackers no longer need to breach a fortress wall; they only need to exploit one unsecured device, one misconfigured microservice, one outdated plugin. Once inside, lateral movement can allow them to access databases, siphon funds, or manipulate credit decisions with alarming speed.

Zero-trust architecture, in contrast, begins with the premise that no user, device, or application should be trusted by default—*even if they are inside the network*. Every access request must be verified, every interaction authenticated, and every action logged and evaluated in real time. Trust becomes dynamic, contextual, and revocable. In the context of digital lending, this shift has profound implications, not only for security, but also for compliance, operational resilience, and borrower confidence.

At the heart of a zero-trust system is continuous identity verification. Unlike static login credentials, which can be stolen or reused, zero-trust frameworks rely on dynamic authentication processes. These include multi-factor authentication (MFA), device fingerprinting, geolocation checks, behavioral analytics, and even biometric inputs. A loan officer accessing underwriting software from their normal IP address on a company-issued laptop may be granted access seamlessly. But the same request from an unknown device, after midnight, from a foreign location, may trigger additional verifications or be blocked entirely. This granular approach to identity ensures that access is tied not just to who someone is, but how and where they are behaving.

For lending platforms, the challenge becomes more complex as operations scale. With remote teams, third-party vendors, embedded finance partners, and cloud-based infrastructures, the number of access points and identities multiplies rapidly. Every new integration or endpoint is a potential vector for compromise. Zero-trust architecture responds by implementing *least privilege access* and *microsegmentation*. Rather than giving employees broad access to databases or administrative tools, users are granted only the precise permissions they need—no more, no less. Infrastructure is divided into granular segments, so even if one part is compromised, the damage is contained. An attacker who gains access to the marketing system, for instance, would find it nearly impossible to pivot into financial records or live transactional environments.

In addition to identity and access control, zero-trust architecture emphasizes real-time monitoring and response. Traditional security systems often operate on batch audits or predefined rules, which can be slow to detect novel threats. Zero-trust platforms, by contrast, integrate with security information and event management (SIEM) systems, machine learning-based anomaly detectors, and behavioral monitoring engines. These tools establish a baseline of normal system activity and continuously scan for deviations—unusual login patterns, anomalous API behavior, or data exfiltration attempts. When anomalies are detected, the system can trigger automatic quarantines, escalate alerts, or revoke session tokens before damage is done.

For digital lending platforms, this real-time vigilance is critical. Consider a scenario in which a botnet attempts credential stuffing attacks on a lending portal. In a perimeter-based model, the system might only detect the breach after significant data exposure. In a zero-trust model, the repeated failed attempts, irregular IP addresses, and velocity of requests would trigger rate limiting, CAPTCHA challenges, and eventually blacklisting. More importantly, even if a credential is successfully stolen, the attacker would face a gauntlet of context-aware security checks before gaining meaningful access.

The architecture also enables better control over **machine-to-machine communication**. In modern lending stacks, data flows constantly between services—credit scoring engines, document verification tools, fraud analytics modules, CRM platforms, and cloud storage providers. Each of these microservices must be authenticated, authorized, and monitored. In a zero-trust environment, mutual TLS (mTLS), service identity tokens, and API gateways enforce strict policies on every interaction. A document upload module cannot query loan databases unless explicitly permitted. An external analytics partner cannot pull raw borrower data without triggering a compliance review. This service mesh approach reduces attack surfaces and makes inter-service abuse far more difficult.

From a regulatory perspective, zero-trust architecture aligns naturally with emerging data protection laws. Regulations like the EU's GDPR, California's CCPA, Brazil's LGPD, and India's DPDP Act require platforms to limit access to personal data, track its usage, and secure it against unauthorized disclosure. Zero-trust systems fulfill these mandates by design. Every data access is logged, purpose-justified, and tied to a traceable identity. Data is encrypted in transit and at rest, and access logs form an immutable trail for audit and legal defense. As regulators demand more proof of proactive governance—especially in financial services—this kind of traceability becomes a strategic asset.

Equally important is **resilience**. A well-implemented zero-trust framework doesn't just prevent breaches—it isolates and absorbs them. If a phishing attack compromises an employee account, the system limits the blast radius. If a vendor's API is abused, access is throttled and revoked without human intervention. These features dramatically reduce the cost and impact of incidents. And in a sector like lending—where downtime can mean lost revenue, delayed approvals, or reputational damage—resilience is not a luxury. It's existential.

That said, adopting zero-trust architecture is not a switch to flip—it's a journey. Many digital lenders are encumbered by legacy systems, fragmented identity providers, or inconsistent data architectures. Implementing zero-trust may require rethinking workflows, refactoring code, upgrading cloud security postures, and retraining staff. It demands buy-in from engineering, operations, compliance, and leadership. It also requires robust endpoint security, because in a zero-trust world, the endpoint is not the edge—it is the frontline. Devices must be hardened, monitored, and enrolled in mobile device management (MDM) or endpoint detection and response (EDR) systems. Policies must enforce encryption, screen locking, patch management, and secure VPN usage.

Moreover, zero-trust should not come at the cost of user experience. Borrowers expect frictionless access, quick onboarding, and instant loan decisions. Striking the right balance between security and usability is the art of modern platform design. Adaptive authentication can help—adjusting security requirements based on risk scores, user behavior, or transaction type. A user with a long, clean history might glide through a loan renewal, while a new applicant from a high-risk IP range is routed through enhanced verification. Security becomes invisible when appropriate and intensive when necessary.

As cyber threats evolve—from ransomware gangs to state-sponsored espionage, from insider threats to supply chain compromises—zero-trust architecture offers a way to meet them with agility rather than fear. It reflects a modern understanding of trust itself: as something that is earned continually, not granted once. For digital lenders, this means never assuming that an authenticated user is who they claim to be, never presuming that a familiar service will always behave ethically, and never allowing past trust to guarantee future access.

In the years ahead, zero-trust will become the default expectation—not just for regulators and technologists, but for borrowers and investors as well. Customers will choose lending platforms that demonstrate robust security practices, especially as data breaches continue to make headlines. Investors will demand cyber risk mitigation as part of due diligence. And regulators will expand their definitions of fiduciary duty to include digital defense. In this environment, zero-trust is not just a technical framework. It is a covenant—between platforms and their users, between data and its stewards, between innovation and responsibility.

Ultimately, the goal of zero-trust security in lending is not paranoia—it's precision. It's about moving from castle-and-moat mentalities to dynamic, intelligent, risk-aware systems that know when to allow, when to deny, and when to question. It's about recognizing that every line of code, every API, every user interaction is a potential gatekeeper of trust. And in a world where trust is the currency of digital finance, protecting it must begin at the architectural level.

9.2 Advanced Fraud Detection Systems

In the ever-expanding landscape of digital lending, fraud is no longer a sporadic threat—it is an ever-evolving adversary embedded deep within the ecosystem. Fraudsters have become more sophisticated, using advanced technology, social engineering, and coordinated networks to exploit system vulnerabilities and manipulate lending platforms. As digital finance becomes increasingly seamless, real-time, and data-driven, lenders must deploy equally advanced fraud detection systems to ensure not just the security of their operations but the long-term trust of their users. Fraud in lending is not merely a matter of financial loss—it is a rupture in the credibility of the platform, and in an environment governed by data, speed, and automation, credibility is the currency that fuels growth.

Traditional fraud detection systems relied heavily on predefined rules. If a borrower applied for multiple loans within a short timeframe, used mismatched addresses, or triggered alerts for high-risk geographies, the system flagged the activity. These rule-based engines served a purpose in an earlier digital era. But fraud is now polymorphic. It learns. It adapts. It finds gaps between rules and moves through them undetected. Identity fraud, synthetic identities, deepfake documents, mule accounts, and malware-infected devices are just a few of the weapons used in this increasingly asymmetric war. A fraudster no longer has to walk into a bank with a fake ID—they can deploy a botnet that creates thousands of identities overnight, all backed by fabricated documentation, with IP masking and behavioral mimicry that would fool any legacy system.

To counter this threat, digital lenders are turning to advanced fraud detection frameworks powered by machine learning, behavioral biometrics, device intelligence, and real-time orchestration engines. These systems do not simply react to red flags; they model risk probabilistically, continuously, and contextually. Instead of hard-coded thresholds, they examine the entire behavioral and data footprint of an application—how fast the form was filled, whether the keystrokes match known patterns, what device is being used, how the mouse moves, whether the phone has been jailbroken, and how the user navigates the site. This behavioral profiling allows platforms to differentiate between legitimate users and bots, between honest applicants and manipulated synthetic identities.

Machine learning models, particularly supervised and unsupervised learning algorithms, play a pivotal role in recognizing patterns that would be invisible to human auditors or static rule engines. Supervised models are trained on labeled data, learning to distinguish fraudulent from legitimate transactions based on historical outcomes. These models evolve as new data arrives, improving their accuracy and reducing false positives. Unsupervised models, on the other hand, excel at detecting novel fraud types—those that have never been seen before. They do this by identifying outliers, anomalies, or clusters of activity that deviate from the norm. For example, a loan application from a device that has never been used before, connecting through a data center proxy, mimicking keystrokes copied from another user session, may pass traditional checks—but would be flagged by an unsupervised model as behaviorally inconsistent.

An equally powerful tool in this ecosystem is the use of cross-institutional intelligence networks. Fraud is rarely isolated to one platform. A user who commits identity fraud at a payday loan provider is likely to attempt the same at a buy-now-pay-later firm or a challenger bank. Advanced fraud detection systems now tap into federated networks that share anonymized fraud signals—device fingerprints, behavioral vectors, email hashes, and transaction patterns—allowing real-time collaboration across the industry. These networks, often operated through consortia or secure blockchain protocols, turn the fragmented efforts of individual firms into a coordinated fraud defense grid. A fraudster blacklisted in Paris can no longer simply pivot to Milan, because their digital footprint has already been flagged, even if their name, IP, or documentation is brand new.

Document and identity verification has also become more advanced through the integration of computer vision and natural language processing. Legacy systems might have simply scanned a passport and compared the name to an application. Modern systems analyze the texture, lighting, hologram reflection, OCR accuracy, and font positioning to verify document authenticity. When combined with liveness detection—such as facial gestures, blink tests, and voice verification—these tools make it exponentially harder for synthetic identities to succeed. The goal is not merely to verify a document, but to verify the human behind it.

Perhaps the most transformative change is the shift from detection to prediction. Advanced fraud systems now aim to understand not just *what happened* but *what is likely to happen.* Using predictive analytics, platforms assess the risk of a user before a transaction is even initiated. If a borrower's device behavior, location, and prior data indicate a high correlation with past fraud clusters, their account might be throttled, limited, or subject to enhanced due diligence. This type of preemptive security aligns with the philosophy of digital lending itself: real-time, data-driven, and intelligent. It's no longer acceptable to catch fraud after funds have left the system—the mandate is to prevent fraud without delaying honest borrowers.

This balance—between security and speed—is where many platforms stumble. Too many false positives lead to borrower frustration, drop-off, and bad reputation. Too many false negatives mean financial loss and reputational damage. The most effective fraud systems are those that operate invisibly in the background, calibrating risk tolerances dynamically, and escalating intervention only when necessary. A one-size-fits-all approach doesn't work in fraud anymore. Context is king. A high-risk signal in one context (e.g., a device reset) may be benign in another (e.g., when paired with verified biometrics).

The future of fraud detection will likely involve even deeper integration of real-time graph analytics, which maps relationships between users, devices, and behaviors across time. Graph models can identify fraud rings, uncover collusion patterns, and surface hidden hierarchies of organized fraud. They visualize the network behind the individual, enabling systems to spot suspicious clusters before a single loan is approved. Coupled with AI co-pilots for fraud analysts, these tools turn raw data into actionable intelligence—fast enough to make decisions at the speed of digital lending.

9.3 Quantum-Resistant Cryptography

If the digital age has taught us one lesson, it is this: the security measures that guard our financial systems today will almost certainly be inadequate tomorrow. This is not a hypothetical concern. The development of quantum computing—a field that once seemed confined to academic theory—has accelerated dramatically in recent years. As research teams move from noisy intermediate-scale quantum (NISQ) devices to fault-tolerant quantum computers, the possibility of breaking today's most commonly used encryption methods moves from improbable to inevitable. For digital lending platforms, which rely on cryptographic protocols to authenticate users, protect data, secure communications, and safeguard transactions, this represents a systemic threat. The answer lies in preparing now—by adopting quantum-resistant cryptography before the day quantum attackers arrive.

Current encryption systems, such as RSA and ECC (Elliptic Curve Cryptography), derive their security from the computational difficulty of factoring large prime numbers or solving discrete logarithmic equations. These problems are virtually insurmountable using classical computers. But quantum machines operating Shor's algorithm could solve them exponentially faster, effectively nullifying the security of most current internet protocols. What today requires billions of years of classical computation could, under quantum attack, take minutes or hours. For lending platforms, this means that encrypted borrower data, if harvested today, could be decrypted retroactively in the future—a tactic known as "harvest now, decrypt later."

This looming threat has galvanized a global movement toward post-quantum cryptography (PQC). The goal is not to build quantum computers, but to defend against them. Quantum-resistant algorithms are designed around mathematical problems

121

that remain hard even for quantum computers. These include lattice-based cryptography, hash-based signatures, code-based systems, multivariate polynomial equations, and supersingular isogeny graphs. Each of these approaches has different strengths in terms of key size, speed, and resilience, but all share one trait: they are immune to known quantum attacks.

For digital lenders, adopting these cryptographic primitives is not just about securing their data—it's about securing the trust architecture that underpins every transaction. If the authentication protocol between a borrower and a platform is compromised, so is the loan agreement. If encrypted communications between back-end services are broken, so is the audit trail. If the ledger integrity of financial transactions is tampered with, so is the validity of the entire system. In a world where credit decisions are increasingly decentralized, instant, and machine-driven, even a momentary lapse in cryptographic assurance could have cascading effects.

Transitioning to quantum-resistant systems is a complex but essential journey. It involves re-architecting key management systems, updating secure sockets layer (SSL/TLS) implementations, migrating encrypted databases, and ensuring backward compatibility with legacy systems. It requires rigorous testing, performance benchmarking, and compliance reviews. Critically, it demands platform-wide readiness—not just from security engineers, but from compliance officers, CTOs, and product managers. Quantum resistance must be seen not as a technical feature, but as a core component of digital lending resilience.

The regulatory environment is beginning to respond. Agencies such as NIST (National Institute of Standards and Technology) have initiated competitions to standardize PQC algorithms, publishing finalists for industry adoption. The NSA has issued guidelines for "quantum-resistant security posture," and financial regulators in the EU and Asia have begun urging critical infrastructure providers—including fintechs—to assess their vulnerability to quantum threats. As part of digital operational resilience (DORA) frameworks and AI governance policies, quantum-readiness may soon become a formal audit requirement.

Some forward-looking lenders are already integrating hybrid cryptographic systems that combine classical and post-quantum algorithms, ensuring that even if one layer is broken, another remains intact. Others are exploring quantum key distribution (QKD), which uses the principles of quantum mechanics to create encryption keys that are theoretically unbreakable—and detectable if intercepted. While still in experimental stages, QKD offers a glimpse of a future where cryptographic security is not just robust, but provably resilient.

The long-term vision is not simply to patch vulnerabilities, but to redesign trust in a quantum-capable world. Just as the transition from physical to digital finance required a reinvention of authentication, identity, and risk, so too will the quantum shift require a reinvention of cryptographic trust. In that world, security will be proactive, mathematically grounded, and futureproofed—not against known threats, but against the very nature of computational progress.

For digital lending platforms, the timeline is clear. Quantum threats are not science fiction—they are a fast-approaching reality. The question is not whether these platforms will need to become quantum-resistant, but whether they will do so before or after a breach. As with all cybersecurity, the cost of prevention is dwarfed by the cost of remediation. And in a financial system where one broken link compromises the whole chain, quantum-readiness is not a feature. It is the foundation of tomorrow's trust.

Chapter 10: The Global Credit Ecosystem: Emerging Markets and Financial Inclusion

10.1 Mobile Money Integration

In many parts of the world, the notion of traditional banking never took root. Brick-and-mortar banks, credit scores, formal loan contracts—these systems, while common in the West, are absent or underdeveloped in large segments of emerging markets. Yet financial life persists, evolves, and in some cases, surpasses conventional models through the rise of mobile money. What began as a means to transfer small amounts of cash via SMS has blossomed into a full-blown financial infrastructure—one that now underpins credit, savings, insurance, and commerce across Africa, Southeast Asia, Latin America, and beyond. Mobile money has not only filled the void left by traditional banking—it has redefined what financial inclusion looks like. And increasingly, it is becoming the bedrock upon which next-generation lending systems are being built.

Mobile money integration refers to the seamless fusion of lending services with mobile-based financial platforms. Unlike in legacy financial ecosystems, where credit requires documentation, collateral, and face-to-face verification, mobile-integrated credit leverages real-time behavioral data, payment history, and mobile usage patterns to deliver tailored financial services to users who may have never stepped inside a bank. This transformation is not just technological—it is deeply cultural, economic, and developmental. It is not about adapting the credit model of developed nations to poorer regions. It is about building a new model entirely—one native to the mobile-first realities of emerging economies.

In Kenya, M-Pesa was the spark that ignited the mobile money revolution. What started in 2007 as a way to send remittances via mobile phones quickly morphed into a national platform for storing value, paying bills, and eventually accessing microloans. Services like M-Shwari, a collaboration between Safaricom and the Commercial Bank of Africa, layered lending capabilities on top of M-Pesa's mobile wallet. Customers with consistent transaction activity and repayment behavior began receiving access to small credit lines. No collateral. No branch visits. No traditional credit score. This model worked because mobile behavior itself became a proxy for trustworthiness.

The integration of mobile money into lending systems creates an entirely new credit underwriting paradigm. Instead of evaluating applicants based on formal income statements or credit bureau data—which many in these regions lack—lenders can assess airtime top-ups, mobile wallet balances, repayment timing on past microloans, the frequency and size of peer-to-peer transfers, and even the usage of mobile data or SMS. Each data point becomes a digital breadcrumb leading toward a holistic credit profile. These alternative indicators, while unorthodox by Western standards, often yield more accurate risk assessments in the contexts where formal financial histories are unavailable or unreliable.

But the benefits of mobile money integration are not confined to data access. It also solves one of the most persistent logistical barriers to lending in underserved regions: distribution. Reaching rural or informal communities with traditional banking infrastructure is costly and slow. Mobile phones, by contrast, are everywhere. In sub-Saharan Africa, mobile penetration exceeds 80%, and in many areas, mobile phones are more accessible than clean water or electricity. Leveraging this ubiquity, mobile-based lenders can instantly disburse funds, collect repayments, and engage borrowers without ever opening a branch. This radically reduces operational costs and allows lenders to serve markets that were once dismissed as commercially unviable.

Moreover, the mobile interface introduces a degree of behavioral design that enhances repayment culture. Push notifications, SMS reminders, USSD prompts—all can nudge users toward timely repayment, reinforce trust, and reduce delinquency. Some platforms have even gamified the experience, rewarding early repayments with larger credit lines or interest rebates. The mobile medium allows lenders to interact not just as banks, but as behaviorally intelligent services that adapt to user needs, preferences, and patterns. In this way, mobile money does not just enable credit—it actively cultivates creditworthiness.

Importantly, mobile money integration is not only transforming lending at the individual level. It is also reshaping how small and microenterprises access capital. In countries where small businesses operate in cash-based, informal economies, gaining access to working capital has historically been a major challenge. Without registered income, legal incorporation, or physical assets, these businesses were invisible to banks. But when a vendor consistently receives mobile payments, purchases inventory using mobile funds, or pays suppliers via phone, that activity becomes a financial identity in its own right. Platforms like Tala, Branch, and Jumo have begun offering microloans to such businesses, underwriting them not through formal paperwork but through mobile money behavior.

This shift has profound implications for development. When small entrepreneurs gain access to credit, they invest in growth. They hire staff, expand inventory, and increase productivity. Numerous studies have shown that access to even modest loans can significantly boost household income, school attendance, and healthcare utilization. Financial inclusion through mobile money is not just about access—it is about empowerment. And credit, when responsibly delivered, becomes a tool for economic mobility.

However, mobile money integration is not without its challenges. One of the most pressing is fraud and identity theft. In regions where SIM cards can be easily cloned or traded, ensuring that the borrower is who they claim to be is a non-trivial task. Many platforms now employ multifactor authentication, liveness checks through front cameras, or partnerships with telcos to triangulate location and usage history. Nonetheless, identity verification remains a persistent risk vector.

Another challenge is pricing. Mobile-based microloans often carry high interest rates—not out of greed, but because default risk, operating costs, and lack of collateral must be absorbed into the loan price. Critics have argued that these rates may border on predatory, especially when compounded by short loan durations and fees. The counterargument, however, is that access to small, high-frequency credit—when used responsibly—can serve as a stepping stone toward more formal financial inclusion. Still, there is a growing consensus that pricing models must evolve, and that financial education must accompany loan disbursement to prevent cycles of debt.

Regulation is also playing catch-up. In many jurisdictions, mobile money exists in a legal gray zone—not fully regulated like banks, but too influential to ignore. Central banks have begun issuing licenses for digital lenders, setting caps on loan rates, and mandating disclosures. This regulation is essential to protect users, ensure interoperability between providers, and foster a competitive ecosystem. The challenge is finding the right balance—regulating without stifling innovation, protecting without centralizing, enabling scale without inviting abuse.

Integration, in this sense, is more than technical. It is systemic. For mobile money to become the backbone of inclusive credit systems, interoperability must extend beyond APIs. It must extend to regulatory harmonization, to shared digital identity frameworks, to cross-platform data portability, and to common ethical standards. Lenders, telcos, governments, and fintech innovators must collaborate to build an ecosystem where trust is embedded, rights are respected, and access is universal.

We are beginning to see early signs of such collaboration. In Ghana, the interoperability of mobile money systems allows users to transfer funds across networks—breaking down silos and encouraging competition. In India, the Aadhaar biometric identity system is being used to verify mobile borrowers and link them to bank accounts. In the Philippines, mobile microinsurance is bundled with mobile lending, offering borrowers a safety net against health or weather shocks. These integrations represent the next frontier—where mobile money becomes not just a payment rail or a loan conduit, but a comprehensive financial platform.

The future of mobile money integration will likely involve deeper personalization, AI-driven credit scoring, embedded finance in e-commerce apps, and programmable money through blockchain-based tokens. Imagine a world where a farmer receives a microloan disbursed directly to her phone, with repayment automatically deducted from crop sales tracked through a mobile agri-marketplace. Or where a gig worker in Lagos builds a credit history through mobile ride payments, qualifying for a motorcycle loan delivered through an integrated logistics platform. These scenarios are no longer fiction—they are pilot programs underway, preparing to scale.

Ultimately, mobile money integration is not just a feature of financial inclusion—it is its engine. It enables credit where banks will not go, empowers people whom the system has overlooked, and establishes a data trail where none existed. It is financial innovation at its most human level: not for efficiency alone, but for equity. Not for disruption's sake, but for development's future. The phone in someone's hand has become more than a communication device—it is a bank, a ledger, a marketplace, and now, a lifeline to credit.

10.2 Microfinance Technology Transformation

Microfinance has long stood as a symbol of hope and progress in the world's underserved regions. Originally conceived as a mechanism for extending small loans to those excluded from formal banking systems—especially women and rural entrepreneurs—microfinance reshaped how the financial industry thought about risk, empowerment, and poverty alleviation. However, the early promise of microfinance was hindered by structural limitations: high operational costs, limited reach, manual processes, and often unsustainable repayment models. For decades, the model struggled to scale, and critics began to question its real impact. But that narrative is now changing—dramatically—through the infusion of technology.

What we are witnessing today is not an evolution, but a reinvention of microfinance, driven by mobile platforms, artificial intelligence, digital identity systems, cloud infrastructure, and real-time analytics. The very architecture of microfinance is being rewritten. Where paper-based ledgers and in-person group meetings once defined the rhythm of lending and repayment, digital interfaces and algorithmic assessments now dominate. Technology is allowing microfinance institutions (MFIs) to do more than digitize old processes—it is empowering them to create new ones altogether, better aligned with the realities of the populations they serve.

One of the most transformative shifts has been the move to fully digital onboarding and loan disbursement. In traditional models, new borrowers often had to meet face-to-face with field officers, provide physical identification, and attend training sessions before qualifying for credit. Today, biometric identity systems—combined with mobile registration platforms—allow users to open microfinance accounts remotely. A fingerprint, iris scan, or national ID number can now unlock access to financial tools. In countries like India, where Aadhaar links biometrics to a centralized digital identity, onboarding can occur in minutes rather than days.

This is particularly important for women and rural dwellers, who have historically faced barriers to accessing financial services—not just due to poverty, but because of geography, social constraints, and systemic discrimination. With smartphones or basic feature phones, they can now engage with microfinance institutions directly, bypassing physical limitations. Technology is removing the gatekeepers that have long mediated their access to capital.

Once inside the system, digital lending tools transform how creditworthiness is assessed. MFIs have traditionally relied on group guarantees—where borrowers form self-monitoring collectives that co-guarantee each other's loans. While effective in some contexts, these models can also breed pressure, conflict, and inefficiency. Technology now allows MFIs to assess individual borrower behavior using alternative data: mobile phone usage, airtime top-ups, mobile payment patterns, business transaction records, GPS movement, and even social media activity. These signals help predict repayment capacity far more accurately than self-reported income or peer recommendations.

Machine learning plays a central role here, modeling borrower risk across thousands of data points that would be unmanageable by human underwriters. These models can identify behavioral patterns—such as regular spending habits or seasonal fluctuations in mobile cash flow—that indicate both opportunity and vulnerability. As these insights deepen, credit offerings can become more personalized: dynamic repayment terms, flexible loan sizes, and targeted financial literacy prompts adapted to the unique life patterns of the borrower.

Digital wallets are another linchpin in this transformation. Once a loan is approved, funds can be disbursed directly into mobile money accounts, where they can be spent, saved, or transferred without incurring the risks or costs associated with cash. This also enables better tracking: repayments can be automated, and missed payments can trigger gentle reminders or restructure offers, reducing default rates and improving transparency.

Technology also solves the problem of scale. MFIs that once relied on a network of local branches and field agents to reach borrowers can now operate nationally—or even regionally—from a centralized digital platform. Loan officers can monitor entire borrower portfolios from a tablet. Mobile apps allow real-time performance tracking, geotagging of field visits, and instant reporting. This operational efficiency not only reduces costs—it allows MFIs to serve more people, in more places, with better service.

Yet perhaps the most profound transformation is not in operations or data, but in accountability. Digital microfinance platforms often incorporate impact measurement tools that track borrower progress beyond loan repayment: changes in income, education access, healthcare spending, or business growth. These metrics help donors, regulators, and development partners evaluate the real social return of lending programs. And because they're digitally gathered, aggregated, and visualized, they provide feedback loops that improve future program design.

That said, the rise of digital microfinance also brings new risks. Over-lending, where borrowers take multiple loans across platforms, is one growing concern—particularly in unregulated digital lending markets. To mitigate this, some countries are building shared credit registries or blockchain-based borrower identity networks to track loan exposure in real time. Privacy is another issue. As microfinance goes digital, borrower data becomes more exposed to breach or misuse. Strong data protection frameworks, ethical use of AI, and borrower education around digital rights are essential safeguards.

Even as MFIs embrace technology, they must not lose sight of the human element. The success of microfinance has always depended not just on capital, but on trust, support, and community. Technology must enhance, not replace, these values. Chatbots can answer common borrower questions, but real people are still needed to counsel, empathize, and resolve nuanced issues. AI can model risk, but it cannot always model grace or generosity. The future of microfinance will be hybrid: digital at its core, human at its heart.

And that future is arriving fast. Across Africa, Latin America, and Asia, MFIs are reinventing themselves as digital-first platforms that serve not just the poor, but the connected, mobile-savvy citizens of the new global South. As smartphones become ubiquitous and data infrastructure strengthens, the barriers that once kept microfinance small and isolated are dissolving. In their place is a new paradigm: agile, scalable, intelligent—and inclusive in ways that traditional banking never imagined.

10.3 Cross-Border Payment Integration

If microfinance addresses the hyper-local needs of underserved communities, cross-border payment integration addresses the global web of financial interdependence that increasingly defines modern economies. In a world where people migrate for work, trade flows across continents, and digital platforms operate transnationally, the ability to send and receive money across borders—instantly, cheaply, and securely—is no longer a luxury. It is a necessity. And yet, for decades, the infrastructure of international payments has remained stubbornly antiquated: expensive, slow, opaque, and exclusionary. The emergence of digital financial technologies, especially in the lending ecosystem, is now rewriting that script.

Cross-border payments have historically been dominated by a handful of legacy institutions—SWIFT, correspondent banks, and remittance giants like Western Union and MoneyGram. While these systems serve a critical role, they are plagued by inefficiencies: multi-day settlements, high transaction fees, unfavorable exchange rates, and compliance bottlenecks. For someone sending money from Nigeria to the Philippines, or from Peru to Bangladesh, the experience is often frustrating and costly. And for small lenders trying to move capital into emerging markets or collect repayments from borrowers abroad, the traditional infrastructure creates barriers that throttle growth.

The digital lending revolution depends on the frictionless flow of capital. Whether it's a peer-to-peer lending platform enabling diaspora communities to fund entrepreneurs in their home countries, or an institutional investor backing a microfinance initiative across borders, payment rails must support real-time, affordable, transparent transfers. To meet this demand, new players and technologies are stepping in—and reshaping the architecture of global finance.

At the forefront is the rise of blockchain-based remittance and settlement networks. Platforms like Stellar and Ripple use distributed ledgers to facilitate nearly instant cross-border payments, settling transactions in seconds at a fraction of the cost of traditional systems. These platforms connect liquidity providers in multiple countries, allowing fiat currencies to be exchanged via crypto-bridging assets or stablecoins, without relying on legacy correspondent banking. The benefits are enormous: reduced cost, enhanced speed, and full traceability.

These advantages matter deeply in the credit space. Consider a scenario where a borrower in rural Uganda secures a microloan from a European crowdfunding platform. In the past, this would require weeks of transfer processing, with large intermediary cuts and currency conversion losses. Today, with blockchain integration, the same transaction can be initiated, cleared, and confirmed within minutes. The lender gains efficiency. The borrower gains trust. And both avoid the hidden taxes of outdated financial plumbing.

But blockchain is not the only innovation driving this change. Mobile money interoperability, as seen in East Africa, allows users to send funds between different providers and across borders. Integration with global fintechs—like TransferWise (Wise), Remitly, or WorldRemit—enables transparent exchange rates and near-instant transfers to bank accounts, digital wallets, or cash pickup locations. These platforms are increasingly embedding themselves into lending systems, allowing repayments to be automated, reconciled, and tracked across jurisdictions.

Digital identity and KYC (Know Your Customer) compliance are key to this evolution. For cross-border payments to scale within regulated environments, identity verification must be portable and robust. Technologies like e-KYC, biometrics, and decentralized identity (DID) frameworks are helping platforms onboard users remotely while meeting global anti-money laundering (AML) standards. This not only streamlines the user experience—it strengthens trust with regulators and partners alike.

Moreover, programmable payments are creating new possibilities. Smart contracts on blockchain networks can automate repayment schedules, escrow arrangements, and even conditional disbursements based on verified milestones—such as business revenue or project completion. This reduces counterparty risk in cross-border lending and enhances transparency for donors, impact investors, and public-private development programs.

The promise of cross-border payment integration also extends to supply chain lending and trade finance. Small exporters in Southeast Asia, for example, can receive upfront financing against future invoices from European fintech platforms, with repayments tied to international payment flows. Farmers in Latin America can obtain input loans funded by buyers in North America, with deductions made at the point of produce sale. These models break down geographic barriers and democratize access to working capital.

Challenges remain, of course. Regulatory arbitrage, currency volatility, capital controls, and data localization laws can still complicate cross-border flows. Institutions must navigate fragmented legal environments, build compliance engines that adapt to multiple jurisdictions, and secure local partnerships for on-the-ground distribution. But momentum is growing, and the strategic imperative is clear: seamless, integrated, and secure cross-border payments are the connective tissue of global credit ecosystems.

In the coming years, we are likely to see more initiatives led by central banks—such as wholesale CBDCs (Central Bank Digital Currencies) or regional payment corridors—designed to enhance interoperability and reduce reliance on dollar clearing. Public-private partnerships will play a critical role, as will open standards and interoperability protocols. The future of inclusive lending depends on this infrastructure maturing—not just within nations, but across them.

As the credit frontier expands, no borrower should be unreachable, and no lender should be held back by borders. Cross-border payment integration, once a technical ambition, is now a moral and economic imperative—linking people, capital, and possibility into a truly global financial web.

Conclusion: Embracing the Credit Revolution

We are standing at the edge of a transformation so profound that most will not even recognize it until it has already swept past them. Business credit, once governed by archaic rules, limited data, and slow-moving institutions, is being redefined in real time. What was once a stifling and exclusive system is now being challenged by technology that knows no borders, algorithms that see patterns beyond human perception, and networks that outpace even the fastest bureaucracy. The revolution in business credit is not simply a story of better underwriting or digital convenience—it is the reorganization of power in the financial world. It is about who gets access, who gets left behind, and how risk and trust are being renegotiated in the language of data.

For decades, access to credit was seen as a reward for already being in the system. If your business had a longstanding relationship with a bank, a consistent history of payments, a thick file of financial statements, and a favorable score from a credit bureau, you were eligible for capital. If you didn't—if you were too small, too new, too unconventional—you were either ignored or penalized. Traditional credit models operated under the assumption that trust had to be proven first. But in a world where innovation outpaces documentation, and where value creation often begins outside of institutions, that model has become obsolete. Businesses can no longer afford to wait for a system that was never designed for them.

The new era of business credit turns that model on its head. It says: trust can be inferred from behavior, not legacy. It says: the past is not always the best predictor of the future. It recognizes that a company's creditworthiness is not frozen in its financial statements, but alive in its real-time data—its sales, its supply chains, its customers, its software. We have entered a time when your payment processing history, your inventory turnover, your mobile wallet activity, or even the uptime of your connected devices can be used to prove that you are worthy of investment. Credit no longer belongs to the few with perfect records—it belongs to the many with momentum, integrity, and digital footprints.

What this revolution demands of us, however, is not passive admiration. It demands active participation. This is not a moment to watch from the sidelines. Whether you are a lender, a business owner, a developer, or a regulator, your role in the emerging credit ecosystem must be deliberate. You must decide what kind of system you want to build—and what kind of future you want to enable. Because the technologies driving this shift are neutral in themselves. Artificial intelligence, blockchain, alternative data, embedded finance, open banking—these are tools. Whether they create liberation or exploitation depends entirely on the ethics, governance, and imagination of the people who wield them.

This book has taken you through that terrain. From the fall of the FICO monopoly to the rise of decentralized credit bureaus. From explainable AI models to quantum-resistant security. From embedded lending in ERP software to the cross-border integration of digital currencies. Each chapter has revealed another piece of the mosaic forming before us—a new vision of what credit can be when it is fast, fair, and intelligent. These are not abstract futures. They are live pilots, scale-ready platforms, regulatory testbeds, and active infrastructures already shaping markets.

But it would be naïve to believe that this future will arrive evenly or without resistance. Legacy institutions do not fade quietly. They fight for control, often cloaking their self-preservation in the language of caution. And rightly so: financial systems, when disrupted recklessly, can produce chaos. But the greater risk lies in defending outdated models under the guise of prudence. In doing so, we risk entrenching inequality and stalling innovation. The goal is not to burn down the old system—it is to rewire it. To take what works—risk awareness, regulatory protections, fiduciary responsibility—and embed those values into systems that are also inclusive, adaptive, and transparent.

One of the most powerful outcomes of the credit revolution is the democratization of access. A small merchant in Jakarta, a logistics startup in Nairobi, a freelancer in Bogotá—each of them can now access funding from institutions they've never seen, in countries they've never visited, based on data that used to be invisible. This is no small shift. It is the globalization of trust. And with it comes new responsibilities. Global credit access requires global safeguards. Data protection laws must be enforced across borders. Algorithmic bias must be audited by diverse actors. And digital identity systems must be interoperable without becoming surveillance tools. The infrastructure of trust must evolve as fast as the infrastructure of finance.

Yet the promise remains extraordinary. With the right safeguards, we can create a world in which a startup in a remote village can access working capital without pledging collateral. A supply chain disrupted by climate events can trigger automatic insurance disbursements based on satellite data. A businesswoman previously excluded from formal banking can build a global credit profile through her e-commerce activity alone. A migrant worker can support a small enterprise back home through tokenized investments verified on a decentralized ledger. These are not fantasies—they are visible on the horizon, waiting to be claimed by those willing to build bridges between data, dignity, and credit.

The platforms that succeed in this new environment will be those that see credit not merely as a transaction but as a relationship.

They will build trust not through opacity but through explainability. They will design not just for scale, but for equity. And they will remember that behind every dataset is a human being trying to build something—be it a family, a company, a dream, or a future. Technology may speed up the process, but it must never replace the purpose.

For business owners, this means embracing transparency and digital agility. It means treating your data as an asset, your online behavior as part of your reputation, and your financial ecosystem as something that extends far beyond your bank. It also means pushing back against systems that grade you unfairly or exclude you without explanation. The revolution gives you tools—but you must wield them wisely.

For lenders, it means leaving behind the comfort of rigid scorecards and embracing the complexity of real-time risk modeling. It means seeing borrowers as partners, not profiles. And it means investing in systems that are both predictive and just. The temptation to optimize only for speed and margin will be strong—but the lenders who win will be those who also optimize for trust and accountability.

For policymakers, the task is both urgent and delicate. Regulation must not suffocate innovation, but neither can it lag behind it. Rules must be designed for systems that are open, modular, and global. They must anticipate not just technological change, but human consequence. Regulators must collaborate across borders, across sectors, and with the very innovators they seek to oversee. Only then can they build a framework where credit is expansive, safe, and resilient.

And for developers, engineers, data scientists—the architects of this new credit infrastructure—the responsibility is perhaps greatest. Every line of code you write is a decision about what is possible, who is included, and how fairness is defined. In your models, lives will be accepted or denied, funded or frozen. It is not enough to optimize for efficiency. You must design for justice.

This credit revolution is not a destination—it is an unfolding process. It will continue to evolve with each technological breakthrough, each regulatory milestone, each behavioral shift. But its direction is clear: toward decentralization, inclusivity, transparency, and speed. Toward a world in which access to credit is not a privilege granted by gatekeepers, but a right inferred from honest participation in the digital economy.

We cannot predict every development that will shape this transformation. But we can choose the principles that will guide it. A commitment to inclusion. A reverence for privacy. A belief in the transformative power of entrepreneurship. And a recognition that technology, when anchored in ethics, can do more than move money—it can unlock potential.

Embracing the credit revolution, then, is not just about adapting to new tools. It is about aligning with a new vision: one where access to capital is faster, fairer, and more human. One where businesses of every size, in every region, are given the chance to grow not because they fit a template, but because they demonstrate real-world value. One where credit is not the end of the journey, but the beginning of something bigger.

The old gatekeepers are falling. The new systems are rising. The choice before us is simple: to cling to the past, or to shape the future. The credit revolution is already here. The question is—what will you do with it?

www.ingramcontent.com/pod-product-compliance
Lightning Source LLC
Chambersburg PA
CBHW070406200326
41518CB00011B/2081